# Tried & Chosen

Published in USA

Library of Congress Cataloging-in-Publication Data

Author Terri Hutchinson

ISBN 978-0-9857712-0-1

Printed in the United States of America

20  19  18  17  16  15 14    1  2  3  4  5  6  7  8  9  10

AN OBSTACLE MEANS THAT GOD
IS GETTING READY TO MAXIMIZE
YOUR HIDDEN POTENTIAL.

REJECTION IS A DIVINE ANNOUNCEMENT
THAT YOU HAVE FINISHED YOUR
WORK IN YOUR CURRENT REALM.

IT TAKES AN OBSTACLE AND A REJECTION
TO AWAKEN YOUR TRUE POTENTIAL.

**Dr. CINDY TRIMM**

# Author

I wrote this book so that my personal testimony could unlock your faith to conquer, overcome, and achieve victory in every type of affliction. I have recorded my thoughts and insights on the matter into this book so that you may know how the rewards of faith are sweet.

# ACKNOWLEDGEMENTS

I would like to express my deepest gratitude to the following people for their magnificent support and contributions to my journey and the creation of this book. To my children Terry, Starr, and Cecil, thank you for your outstanding understanding. I give honor to my Mom and Dad for training me to be a leader. A special thank you to Dwight and Sherice Pickens for your tremendous financial support through the years. To my sister Elizabeth Hutchinson, my live-in nurse; thank you for making me laugh through the pain. Lori Young—Wow! To the Duffey family, I fully appreciate your analytical approach to everything. Nini Treadwell, I love you. Ann Claybon, you are the best. To Quint Harris, thank you for believing in me, supporting me, and teaching me.

With deep gratitude I wish to thank every person who has come into my life and inspired, touched, and enlightened me through their presence. May God Bless you in every way.

# DEDICATION

This book is first dedicated to that chosen believer who needs the days ahead to be better than the days gone by.

This work is further dedicated to the late Wilhemina Harrington (1902-2011). You ordained and catapulted my ministry into what it has become today. I am flying like an eagle.

# FOREWARD

As I read this book I come away with realizing that the author has such an amazing revelation of knowledge and understanding.

This book is an excellent resource for your personal library and for those of us who minister because it has practical and spiritual applications that can be used as a reference for anyone who is dealing with various afflictions.

God has used this author in such a profound way to tap into the struggles of everyday people whether they are Christians or not.

You will be encouraged and inspired after reading this book because iron sharpens iron and from time to time, we find our swords have gotten dull as we face the adversities of life.

Not only is the book encouraging but it is also scripture based, listing scriptures that are directly related to many of these afflictions and for me that is what I look for when reading books.

Pastor Debbie Banks
Assistant Pastor
Spirit of Life Christian Fellowship
Riverside, CA

# Descriptions and Definitions

**Adversity** - a state of hardship, difficult circumstances; misfortune

**Affliction** - a state of pain or distress; that which causes suffering; a misfortune, a calamity

**Calamity** - extreme misfortune; tragedy

**Dark** - lacking or having very little light

**Difficult** - requiring considerable effort; hard to accomplish, endure, please, understand, etc.; hard to deal with or satisfy

**Distress** - suffering, such as pain, anxiety, discomfort, etc.; a condition requiring immediate help

**Desert** - a dry, often sandy, barren region

**Gazingstock** - to be made a spectacle of; a reproach others look down upon

**Hardship** - any difficulty

**Midnight** - the middle of the night, the transition time period from one day to the next: the moment when the date changes

**Ordeal** - a trying experience

**Painful** - disagreeable sensation caused by injury

**Predicament** - a situation—especially an unpleasant, troublesome, or trying one—from which extrication is difficult

**Privation** - abject poverty

**Shadow** - comparative darkness caused by interruption of light; the image produced by that which interrupts light

**Sickness** - affected by disease; weak; emotionally upset

**Sore straits** - anything causing pain or trouble going through a narrow passage

**Struggle** - an arduous effort; a war; to contend with adversity

**Suffering** - to sustain loss or injury; to endure

**Trial** - examination in a court of law; the process of testing, hardship

**Tribulation** - a cause for distress or suffering

**Valley** - an area drained by a river; low land lying between mountains or hills; a hollow

**Winter** - the coldest season

**Wilderness** - an uncultivated or uninhabited area

**War** - armed strife between nations, states, etc.; any conflict or struggle

# Contents

# INTRODUCTION

This book is about standing. Standing in the love of God, standing on the Word of God and standing on the promises of God requires that you stand in faith. Standing in faith is vital to your survival in the kingdom of God. Those that have been chosen to complete an assignment, a task, a mission, or a mandate by God often find themselves under attack in some way or another every day. The enemy is always on the prowl to persecute the chosen believer. Do you want to know why bad things happen to good people? Well, stay tuned because this book will give you answers. Answers to "Why" will be demystified. You will learn to stand and defend yourself with the whole armor of God and know that only through a personal intimate relationship with God will you truly comprehend His promise to never leave you nor forsake you. I will give you biblical understanding concerning your life as a chosen Christian in terms of victory and deliverance from pain, hardship, and adversity. My assignment is to give you helpful instruction on how to endure affliction by deepening your relationship with the Lord Jesus Christ. You will receive encouragement as you realize the power you possess to stand.

When God desires for you to experience a new level of worship, He calls you into a deeper relationship with Him. This call gets the attention of the devil and that's when things seem to go haywire. This is a signal that a call has been made on your spirit. The devil puts out an All Points Bulletin on you. You make the most wanted list. When you begin to worship God, you make yourself susceptible to the cleansing power of the Holy Spirit. You will be tried.

In order for you to go higher in God, He tends to go deeper into you, and it starts with a desire He places in your heart to serve Him more. This elevated status requires a refining process. The devil seems to know it and even be involved in it. You have been chosen.

The concept of affliction is over flowing with meaning, making it necessary to view it from different angles to fully grasp it. The terms of affliction that I use are interchangeable to describe difficult places in our Christian experiences.

As you read this book, you will gain an understanding for the reasons you go through trials and tribulations. You will also receive greater insight into why you experience difficult "light afflictions." Rightly dividing the word for you to receive an impartation is my goal as you become more aware of and knowledgeable in your soul and spirit concerning the things of God and the ways of God. Some truths I explore will definitely take your mind to new depths of mystery and revelation. This book will inspire you to get through tough times. Whenever God's in the process of doing something new in your life, He starts breaking down everything from the past, causing you to exercise trust and faith for your future. (See Jeremiah 1:10.) When you give your tried and chosen testimony, your words will have more power and God will get more glory.

In this book I also describe in clear detail the endurance necessary for the times and seasons of a chosen believer's spiritual growth. I will show you the value of endurance in overcoming personal challenges and teach you to find inner strength. I include references to experiences in my own life as a testimony. I looked carefully at my affliction in order to gain understanding of *why*, and I want you too to look carefully at your own life and hardship to understand your *why*. Spiritual growth is a lifetime journey and I now know the why and the way.

You will be amazed at the faithfulness of God. This book will help you "get fortified" and prepare you for the endurance you must stand on. For in due season your prayers, your waiting, and your tears will have been answered.

*For so an entrance shall be ministered unto you abundantly into the everlasting kingdom of our Lord and Savior Jesus Christ.*

*Wherefore I will not be negligent to put you always in remembrance of these things, though ye know them, and be established in the present truth.*

*Yea, I think it meet, as long as I am in this tabernacle, to stir you up by putting you in remembrance.*                    **—2 Peter 1:11-13**

*And the afflicted people thou wilt save.*                    **—2 Samuel 22:28a**

*Chaos is disorder that sets the stage for the next season of order.*

"EVERYTHING IN THE KINGDOM OF GOD OPERATES BY FAITH, BUT FAITH WON'T WORK WITHOUT LOVE."

*Creflo Dollar*

# GOD IS LOVE

*And we have known and believed the love that God hath to us. God is love; and he that dwelleth in love dwelleth in God, and God in him.*
*—1 John 4:16*

The Song of Songs, more wonderful than any other love poetry, was composed by King Solomon. This song expresses God's love poem for you. It is a beautiful story about pursuing you in love, expressing love to you and enjoying the glory of wedded love. Your relationship with God is sacred. God set forth the love that Christ has for the church—Christ as groom and the Church as bride. You are the bride because you are the church. True love is worth pursuing and it should be expressed with passion. The above Scripture encourages us to dwell in love—to live in love. This means you must abandon yourself wholeheartedly, holding nothing back. God is chasing you with zeal and wooing you with tenderness to win your heart. (See Song of Solomon 4: 1-15.)

*And as we live in God, our love grows more perfect. So we will not be afraid on the day of judgment, but we can face him with confidence because we are like Jesus here in this world.*        *—1 John 4:17* NLT

So we will not be ashamed and embarrassed, as Adam and Eve were after the fall in the garden, but shall face Him with confidence and joy, because He loves us and we love Him too. There is no need for us to be afraid of someone who loves us perfectly and unconditionally. In my relationship with my three children, it is fully known to them that they can come to me with the good, the bad, and the ugly. The love of God eliminates all dread and expels every trace of terror. When you are fully convinced that God really does love you, you will not be afraid of correction. This confidence comes with full maturity of love. What do I mean by full maturity of love? Dwelling in love on purpose by being kind, patient, hopeful, and humble. Love is seen in our behavior toward one another. As we live with Christ, our love grows more perfect and complete. It is by our love that the world will know we are believers. Everything in the Kingdom of God operates by love, and since faith works by love, it is love that forms a foundation for faith. The faith to come to God whenever, however, and whatever.

*There is no fear in love; but perfect love casteth out fear: because fear hath torment. He that feareth is not made perfect in love.*
*—1 John 4:18*

God is love, and this means that His essential nature is love. God will never act contrary to His nature. You will never experience God expressing His will except in a demonstration of perfect love. God's kind of love always seeks His best for each person. If we reject His best, He will discipline us. However, the discipline will come from a heavenly Father who loves us and who will do whatever is necessary to bring us to a place in our lives where we can receive what He wants to give us.

*In the distant future, when you are suffering all these things, you will finally return to the Lord your God and listen to what he tells you. For the Lord your God is a merciful God.* *—Deuteronomy 4:30-31 NLT*

God must draw us in to Him, wooing us and leading us to be closer to Him.

*And have you [completely] forgotten the divine word of appeal and encouragement in which you are reasoned with and addressed as sons? My son, do not think lightly or scorn to submit to the correction and discipline of the Lord, nor lose courage and give up and faint when you are reproved or corrected by Him.* *—Hebrews 12:5 AMP*

Tucked away in the midst of the romance of the Song of Songs is an extremely valuable piece of wisdom for everyday life: it is "the little foxes" that spoil the vine (see Song of Solomon 2:15), meaning that peoples' lives are not typically destroyed by what we would consider "big" issues, but by a series of smaller, seemingly insignificant choices or compromises.

*And ye have forgotten the exhortation which speaketh unto you as unto*
*children, My son, despise not the chastening of the Lord, nor faint when*
*thou are rebuked of Him: for whom the Lord loveth He chasteneth,*
*and scourgeth every son whom He receiveth. If ye endure chastening,*
*God dealeth with you as with sons; for what son is he whom the Father*
*chasteneth not?* —Hebrews 12:5-7

When looking at your situation and viewing your circumstances, keep in mind the cross, where God clearly demonstrated once and for all His deep love for us. God gave His Son. You may not always understand your current situation or how things will eventually turn out, but you can trust in the love Christ proved to you when he laid down His life for you on the cross. In the death and resurrection of Jesus Christ, I am forever convinced that God loves me. So I say to you, choose to base your trust in God on what you know for sure— His love for you—and choose to trust that, in time, He will help you understand the confusing circumstances you may be experiencing.

God seeks a close, one-on-one relationship with You and me. God does not want us to merely believe in Him, He wants to relate to us on a personal level. He does not just want to hear us recite prayers. He wants to converse with us. The plan is to be actively involved in our lives each and every day. God knows what your life can become. Only He understands your full potential as His own child. He does not want you to miss out on any good thing He has for you. He wants you to have an intimate love relationship with Him that is real and personal.

*And this is life eternal, that they might know thee the only true God, and Jesus Christ, whom thou hast sent.*                    —*John 17:3*

Believers can be in many different places along their spiritual walk. Some of us are 10 meters from our destination and some of us are miles away. We are all walking with help from the Holy Spirit. The Holy Spirit is there as your teacher to teach you and guide you into all truth. The truth of God's love will grow deeper and stronger as you yield to the promptings and leadings of the Holy Spirit.

There is a world of difference between knowing something to be true in your head and experiencing the reality in your life. Believers will say they know that God loves them because the Bible tells them so, however, when you have been tried and chosen, you gain experiential understanding of God as your lover. You find out that God does not merely want you to read about His love—meaning you understand the concept in your mind—He also wants you to love Him by experience. When you have a love relationship with God, you will experience Him actively working in and through your life.

God is the great "I AM." This means that He will be whatever you need Him to be in your life. For example, you could not truly know God as the "Comforter in sorrow" unless you experience His compassion during a time of grief or sadness. The various names of God found in Scripture can become a call to worship for you as you call out for what you need. The names of God reveal something of His nature, activity, or character. In this chapter, I want you to understand His love nature, and throughout this book we will be calling on His names to indicate we are seeking His presence and acknowledging that we know Who He is.

Love is the driving force behind giving. God shows His love by giving. His greatest gift to the world is recorded as "'His only be-gotten son," Jesus Christ. God also gives hope, deliverance, victory, peace, and joy to name a few. God, in His great love gave believers commands to keep. These commands are not grievous and when kept provide safety and protection. You come to know and love God by experience—at His initiation—as He allows you to learn something new about His love for you. As you experience God, you grow in your knowledge and love for Him and you will naturally want to express your love with gratitude, praise, and worship. God's love is majestic and worthy of our praise. Show your love by giving God glory.

*"Those who accept my commandments and obey them are the ones who love me. And because they love me, my Father will love them. And I will love them and reveal myself to each of them."*     *—John 14:21* TLB

As believers we must adjust our lives to keep the commands of God. This is seen as evidence that you love Him. Let God love you and teach you about His love as He works through you. If for any reason you think too low of yourself because you have fallen short on a command or two, remember how love is expressed in giving. God gives mercy and He gives grace as you grow spiritually. Paul said God deliberately seeks out the weak and the despised things because it is from them that He receives the greatest glory. (See 1 Corinthians 1:26-31.) When God does exceptional things through unexceptional people, then others recognize that only God could have done it. If you feel weak, limited, and ordinary, take heart. You are the best material through which God can work. When people see real love, they see God. God pursued us and expressed His love with the passion of the Christ.

*We love him, because he first loved us.*     *—1 John 4:19*

## Overflow Scripture Meditations

*God so loved the world, that he gave his only begotten Son.*
—*John 3:16*

*By this shall all men know that ye are my disciples, if ye have love one to another.* —*John 13:35*

*Herein is love, not that we loved God, but that He loved us, and sent His son to be the propitiation for our sins.* —*1 John 4:10*

*Now before the feast of the passover, when Jesus knew that his hour was come that he should depart out of this world unto the Father, having loved his own which were in the world, he loved them unto the end.*
—*John 13:1*

*But faith which worketh by love.* **Galatians 5:6b**

*But as it is written, Eye hath not seen, nor ear heard, neither have entered into the heart of man, the things which God hath prepared for them that love him.* —*1 Corinthians 2:9*

THE MOST IMPORTANT THING IS
THIS: TO BE ABLE AT ANY MOMENT
TO SACRIFICE WHAT WE ARE  FOR
WHAT WE COULD BECOME.

*Charles Dubois*

# WHAT TIME IS IT?

*There is a time for everything, a season for every activity under heaven. A time to be born and a time to die. A time to plant and a time to harvest. A time to kill and a time to heal. A time to tear down and a time to build up. A time to cry and a time to laugh. A time to grieve and a time to dance. A time to scatter stones and a time to gather stones. A time to embrace and a time to turn away. A time to search and a time to quit searching. A time to keep and a time to throw away. A time to tear and a time to mend. A time to be quiet and a time to speak up. A time to love and a time to hate. A time for war and a time for peace.*
*—Ecclesiastes 3:1-8* NLT

In time, there comes a time for you to be moved from one place in God to another place in Him. This is a time of transition and just like the caterpillar which struggles and squirms during his transition, you also will have to deal with a struggle and a squirm. Change happens from time to time, and it may be time to change your name.

Why do I say, "It may be time for a name change?" Because the Bible records several name changes. God does the changing, and if your name had a certain stigma attached to it, you may be next in line for a name change. God changed Sarai to Sarah. Sarah's old name was associated with barrenness. God changed Saul's name to Paul. Paul's old name was associated with murder. God changed Jacob to Israel and Abram's name to Abraham.

A spiritual conflict arose in Sarai before her name was changed. She laughed mockingly when the angel told he she was to birth a son. Sarai knew she was well past the age to bare a child. Also Saul met with spiritual conflict on the road to Damascus before his name was changed.

A spiritual conflict will arise and serves as a signal that you are entering into a transitional time. Transition means that you will be going from one time to another time. Get used to it because this is how God moves you from one season to another season—from good to better. We are reminded not to be troubled and that these things must come to pass . As they do, know that this is not the end, but the beginning of newness. There is more life to come. The invisible is about to become visible, and what you do not know is about to be revealed. Although things may get crazy, you must survive the transition. Saul was struck blind during his transition and made it to a street called Straight. It was dark for him and he had to be led. Likewise when it gets dark for us, we must be led by the Holy Spirit— our guide. New territories you have been chosen to trail blaze are waiting. Nothing will look familiar, and there will be no landmarks as you travel through this time.

You will find yourself in the middle of the water not being where you were and not being where you are going to be. When this time comes you have to make up your mind to go where no man has gone before. There will be decrease before there is increase.

As I was going through my season of affliction, I kept meditating on prophesies that had been spoken over my life and ministry— promises I reminded God of while I was afflicted. My circumstances were contradicting my promises. I was neither here nor there. Before my affliction started, every thing promised was right in front of me and I was very happy. In just a few months, everything came crashing down. I was led into the wasteland like Job. I had to keep telling myself that I heard from God, I knew I did, I had to be in His perfect will for my life. I knew that my relationship with God was steady. In spite of that knowledge, I began to ask myself, "What sin needs to be removed? Am I going higher in God? Why is this happening to me now, right when I have it going on? Am I being tested to stay faithful? Am I being tempted to give up? Does God need to undo the works of the devil? Shall I resist the contradiction happening right now? What time is it?"

I had my goals and promises written down and taped to my wall—so that I may read them and run with them. When the affliction came in waves—oh yes, it was one thing after another—I did what Jesus did when He had been led into the wilderness. I said, "It is written," and quoted the promises God made to me by the Scriptures and by His voice. (See Luke 4:1-12.) This was the right thing to do, because it is exactly what Jesus did when the devil worked on Him for 40 days and 40 nights. This temptation came right after a high point in His spiritual life. He was about to birth forth into His own ministry and fulfill the purposes and plans of God. His cousin, John the Baptist, had just declared that Jesus was the son of God, baptized Him in the Jordan River, and the heavens opened up. Then God spoke confirming what John said and declaring how pleased He was with Jesus. When we are at a high point with God, the devil sees this as a good time to tempt us as well.

Pressure to act ungodly is a temptation you can fight with spoken words, words God has written. However, when I became sick in my body, I could barely talk back to the devil. My health was on the line, I had no song, no strength, no fight, just moans. I was really in the secret place of God—I had to be. The temptation to give up was making the noise of war in my mind and in my emotions. The natural part of me was at an all-time low, but the divine part of me was at an all-time high, because God has you covered when you lay helpless. A transition was taking place in my life.

As chosen believers, we must understand that there is a time for transition from one realm into another realm like when a pregnancy is about to give birth. The baby is in transition from one dimension into another dimension. The water breaks (breakthrough) and you have entered the time of labor. This is the transition which is painful and hard, but absolutely necessary for victory. It was good to be pregnant, but it is better to give birth. This is the time to stand on what God has promised. You will decrease in strength before you increase in victory.

*My God, My God, why have You abandoned Me [leaving Me helpless, forsaking and failing Me in my need]?*          —*Matthew 27:46* AMP

When I gained my strength back after having been tried with sickness, I looked up every Scripture I could get my hands on about affliction. I have included all of them in this book as a testimony and hope to God's chosen believers. During this time of study—oh yes, it was time for me to study what I went through. I first had to understand the value of affliction. Looking back over how sick I was, God began to add healing Scriptures to me and I was healed. Another thing I suffered was a loss of money. And yes, He added financial Scriptures to me. I rediscovered He was my provider!

Whatever the need is, God provides new and old Scriptures to your soul and your spirit. Some verses are brought back to your remembrance and some you hear for the first time. No matter what, God provides you with timely verses for you to stand on for complete victory.

*It is good for me that I have been afflicted, that I might learn Your statutes.*          —*Psalm 119:71* AMP

Understanding that there is value and purpose for sickness does not make the experience feel good. I was sick in my body for over twelve months without clear reasons to the naked eye. I had to endure CAT scans, MRI's, and ultra sounds, but I knew in my knower that God was protecting me. Your knower will make you stand stronger and firmer in the things of God, and your prayer life will be strengthened and cause you to search deeply and more consistently in the Word of God. I held on tightly while facing the fear that creeps in. What the enemy means for evil, God can turn around and make it good. I indeed wanted to learn and understand why affliction was necessary and kept digging into scripture to gain more and more of God.

*And you shall hear of wars and rumors of wars: see that ye be not troubled: for all these things must come to pass, but the end is not yet.*
—*Matthew 24:6*

Conflict, grief, destruction, loss, sorrow, pain, suffering, and death all come to mind when you hear of war. The war that I am speaking of occurs right there in your mind. The enemy brings the fight to you, and your mind is the battlefield. The Bible tells us that we are warriors, and soldiers, and that we are more than conquerors.

This is not something you automatically know. You have to be taught who you really are. To be taught means you will be trained and you will come face-to-face with a battle. As a soldier on the battlefield you will be responsible for carrying out orders, instructions, and or strategies. It takes a mature person to receive instruction and obey. This requires you to recognize that the anointing you are carrying is bigger than the person you are. You are a soldier in God's army. There is a time for war. Since there is a time for war, know that there is also a time for peace.

*Everyone enjoys giving good advice, and how wonderful it is to be able to say the right thing at the right time!*     —*Proverbs 15:23* TLB

There is a right time for everything, and everything has its season. When you face opposition, you are facing promotion. The devil knows you are about to be promoted in the things of God and will oppose you to keep you from standing. Take, for instance, the hatred and taunting you deal with when clearly you are chosen, loved, and favored.

Hannah was loved deeply by her husband Elkanah and Peninnah knew this while producing child after child for him. When Hannah had reached an all time low, she went into the temple to pray. She did not just pray; she prayed hard; she travailed in prayer. Adversity will drive you to God. It drove Hannah to agonize in prayer that day. Eli the priest heard her deep sincerity which caused him to prophesy that her petition was granted. (See 1 Samuel 1.)

The story of Joseph also tells us how opposition arises from close family. Joseph knew from a dream what God had for him, and he shared this with his brothers. We must be careful with whom we share God's revealed plan for our life. Sometimes people will oppose you just because God desires to bless you. Joseph's brothers hated him because of the deep love and favor he received from his natural father. They even more so hated him because of the favor he received from his heavenly Father.

When you have made a total commitment to the Lord, God will give you a glimpse of the magnitude of the blessing that is about to come into your life. The devil will plot to stop the blessing from reaching you; however, God will make known to you the plans of the devil and give you strategies to triumph over him. We just have to let time do what time does. In order to move from one life season to another, change must occur. Every transition encourages our spiritual wholeness and growth. This growth brings glory to God. Repent for any impatience as you wait for God's perfect timing.

*What profit remains for the worker from his toil? I have seen the painful labor and exertion and miserable business which God has given to the sons of men with which to exercise and busy themselves.*

*—Ecclesiastes 3:9* AMP

We indeed are busy. When you have been chosen to complete a task for God, you will be busy. We think we need to know what comes next in our lives and God does not always tell us the next step. God expects us to take our steps by faith. God has also promised us that if we walk uprightly, He will not withhold a good thing. When the time comes for us to cast away stones, remember that there will be a time to gather stones together. For this reason, do not listen to negative reports about your life, health, ministry, family, or calling. When things look to be out of control, well-meaning friends, associates, and family members will try to convince you that they know what is going on with you and God. Jesus says that we ought to pray for these friends, as Job did.

*When Job prayed for his friends, the Lord restored his fortunes. In fact, the Lord gave him twice as much as before!*     *—Job 42:10* NLT

In troubled times, the last thing you want to hear are negative words about you and your circumstance. There is a remedy for this type of behavior, and a strategy to overcome any bitterness you may want to hold on to. Judge the statement, judge the comment, or judge the sin and not the person. Know that it is the enemy using people to oppose you. Pray for them because they may not be aware of Satans' plan to use them.

*But I say unto you, love your enemies, bless them that curse you, do good to them that hate you, and pray for them which despitefully use you, and persecute you.*     *—Matthew 5:44*

God often made references to trees to describe His children. You can tell how old a tree is by counting the rings in the tree's trunk. The rings are dark circles signifying a growth period. They speak of standing the test of time and surviving adverse weather changes.

This brings me to another time in a believer's life, pruning: Jesus makes a distinction between two kinds of pruning: it is a cutting back of branches or a removal of the superfluous branches. There is a time for pruning. You shall find peace when you appreciate God's perfect timing in your life. This pruning improves the shape of the tree, and God's pruning improves the shape of your character. Each season of pruning encourages growth, increases fruitfulness, and makes the fruit in our lives easier to reach. We want our fruit to be easy for others to reach because of the command Jesus gave "be fruitful and multiply." Fruit trees are cut back to promote the proper kind of growth. In other words, sometimes God must discipline us to strengthen our character and faith.

*Every branch in me that beareth not fruit He taketh away: and every branch that beareth fruit, He purgeth it, that it may bring forth more fruit.*                                                                —*John 15:2*

When we survive pain and adversity in our lives, we are left with markings that say, "I was wounded, I endured, I stood, and I survived. Here are the rings to prove it." These markings are the Christ-like characteristics that are developed in us as a result of surviving hardship. They are reminders that say, "I've been tried and chosen." You can look at a fine piece of furniture made from the wood of a tree and see that the more rings or dark circles, the more beautiful the furniture is. Wood veneer, which is man's attempt to capture and reproduce the real beauty of natural wood, can not even come close in comparison.

The trials and tribulations we go through prune us. Spiritual pruning cuts away the superficiality in our lives. We may not even be aware of what is hindering our growth; therefore we must trust God when things go haywire.

*Moreover [let us also be full of joy now!] Let us exult and triumph in our troubles and rejoice in our sufferings, knowing that pressure and affliction and hardship produce patience and unswerving endurance. And endurance (fortitude) develops maturity of character (approved faith and tried integrity). And character [of this sort] produces [the habit of] joyful and confident hope of eternal salvation.* —**Romans 5:3-4** AMP

The above Scripture sounds great, however most of the time I was saying this;

*Bow down Your ear to me, deliver me speedily! Be my Rock of refuge, a strong Fortress to save me.* —*Psalm 31:2* AMP

And;

*Hide not Your face from me in the day when I am in distress! Incline Your ear to me; in the day when I call, answer me speedily.* —*Psalm 102:2* AMP

When everything looks to be falling apart, fear will try to overtake you. I heard a preacher say this about fear: it is *False Evidence Appearing Real.* To overcome fear you must stand in love. You must stand in the faith of love and watch God demonstrate His power over everything that the enemy tries to do. Rely on the love of God to cast out any and all fear that tries to creep into your soul and spirit. In 1 John 4:18, the Bible tells us that "perfect love casteth out fear."

It is important to know and understand what time it really is. Saul, who was well known as a threat to the disciples of the Lord, met with time on his way to the city of Damascus. His mission was to bring any disciples of the Lord, man or woman, back to Jerusalem in chains. Jesus met Saul on the road to tell him it was time for a change. Jesus already knew it had been difficult for Saul to persecute his believers by stating "it is hard for thee to kick against the pricks." Saul had a spiritual conflict in his duty to slaughter the saints of the Lord. However he did it anyway and was good at it. Jesus shined the heavenly light on him causing him to fall down to the ground. When Jesus told him to 'Arise' he rose up converted to Paul, a new man with a new mission in life. Paul had been chosen to go to a new and higher dimension.

*But the Lord said unto him, Go thy way: for he is a chosen vessel unto me, to bear my name before the Gentiles, and kings, and the children of Israel: For I will shew him how great things he must suffer for my name's sake.*                                    —*Acts 9:15-16*

In the beginning when God created the heavens and earth, He designed the earth with four natural seasons: spring, summer, fall, and winter. Each season is marked by certain changes. These natural changes occur to let us know it is time for a new season. The seasons are going to come around whether you are prepared or not. It is important for us to flow with the seasons, and why not flow with what God is doing?

Spring brings many things

Bees and blossoming trees

Birds calling

Rain softly falling

As it passes

Over the grasses

Let me whisper in your ear

Spring is here

*Author unknown*

Next comes summer, summertime is hot. Every one is excited in the summer, golfers, surfers, swimmers, hikers and rock climbers to name a few. Activity is at an all time high. Love and fun in the sun, romance and starry nights are highlighted during this season.

When fall rolls in there is a chill in the air. Our focus changes and the days are shorter, the nights are longer. Activity has slowed down and pretty golden/orange/yellow leaves are every where.

Winter shows up and it is time to hibernate. Beautiful white snow covers the mountains and blankets the ground. The winds blow to clear the air and scatter debris.

I HEARD A BIRD SING

I heard a bird sing

In the dark of December

A magical thing

And sweet to remember:

"We are nearer to Spring

Than we were in September,"

I heard a bird sing

In the dark of December.

*Oliver Herford*

Just like the natural seasons that bring natural changes, spiritual seasons bring about spiritual changes. When you first give your life to Christ you are a babe on the milk of the scriptures. That is a season. As you began to learn of the statutes, the commandments, and the precepts, you go through a different season. Once your walk and your talk changes you have entered into another season. One day you will not speak as a child and will put childish things away and go on to eating the meat of the scriptures. By now you have gone through seasonal changes in your growth with the Lord.

Sometimes change is frustrating and upsetting because it messes up our comfort level. We do not like being uncomfortable. We like our comfort zone. I like the story I heard a preacher tell about the eaglet. When a mother eagle has her nest of eaglets, it is very comfortable with all the things she has gathered to the nest for them. There comes a time when she starts throwing out the twigs of comfort to prepare them for their next level in life. She then takes them out on a branch and pushes them off. The eaglets cannot fly yet, but they are about to start flying lessons. She catches them and does this over and over again taking them to a higher branch, meaning things are getting scarier and more fearful. She continues to catch them as she pushes them off the branch, and then suddenly the eaglet flaps its wings and begins to fly.

Likewise, you too will be a comfortable Christian, going to church singing and making a joyful noise telling everyone about how great your church is and then suddenly, the Holy Spirit will lead you into a dry and desolate place where there is no rest, relief, or comfort. When this happens, God is doing a new thing in your life. You will know the approach of this season. God will reveal to you that things are about to change. It is a spiritual season that you must pass through.

*But forget all that-it is nothing compared to what I am going to do. For I am about to do a brand-new thing. See, I have already begun! Do you not see it? I will make a pathway through the wilderness for my people to come home. I will create rivers for them in the desert!*
*—Isaiah 43:18-19* NLT

Major adjustments have to be made when a promotion is in the making. Significant adjustments are required when God is taking you higher. These adjustments may relate to your thinking, your circumstances, your relationships, your commitments, your actions, and your beliefs. To move you from your way of thinking and acting to God's way of thinking and acting, fundamental adjustments are required. You can't stay where you are and go with God at the same time. You have to be convinced God can do everything He said He would.

In the Bible we are told to test every spirit by the Spirit of God. This will reveal to you where the trouble is coming from, whether it be of God or not. (1 John 4:1). Jesus warned us that there would be trouble in this life and you will want to know where the trouble is coming from. You need the help of the Holy Spirit to test the source of trouble. This will help you in submission to correction, or action into war. This also is a process of faith in God by the Spirit. As we walk by faith, one step at a time.

*In the world ye shall have tribulation.*      *—John 16:33b*

God is always working in the earth realm to accomplish His divine purposes. God did not create the world and then abandon it to run itself. He is not sitting in a heavenly throne room passively observing the activities on earth. God is orchestrating history. He is present and in the middle of all human activity. God is actively at work redeeming a lost world, and He chooses to involve you and me in carrying out His redemptive plans. (2 Corinthians 5:17-20)

When the time comes for you to join God on a higher level, the change produces a new you and a new way for you to work in the kingdom. In Isaiah 6:19 Isaiah realized he had a sinful, unclean mouth that needed to be dealt with. God sent help. The Seraphim came forward with a coal of fire an instantly he was changed, and sometimes God will put us through a cleaning process. The call, the anointing and the appointment can occur in different time periods, but no matter how they take place or in what order, the process of preparation is important. God develops your ambassadorial role for the kingdom. You are representing Him and working with Him.

*We are Christ's ambassadors, and God is using us to speak to you. We urge you, as though Christ himself were here pleading with you, "be reconciled to God!"*          *—2 Corinthians 5:20* NLT

Everyone has their own journey in life, no two are alike. Believers in Christ all learn at different paces, however our step by step guide is the same God today, yesterday, and tomorrow. He will show you your way. God is telling you to lift up and look from where you are (Genesis 13:14-15). Your appointed time has arrived (Habakkuk 2:2-3.) God is continually transforming us into His very own image.

*So all of us who have had that veil removed can see and reflect the glory of the Lord. And the Lord—who is the Spirit—makes us more and more like him as we are changed into his glorious image.*     *—2 Corinthians 3:18* NLT

## Overflow Scripture Meditations

*For the L*ORD *God is a sun and shield: the L*ORD *will give grace and glory: no good thing will he withhold from them that walk uprightly.*     *—Psalm 84:11*

*Thou art worthy, O Lord, to receive glory and honor and power: for thou hast created all things, and for thy pleasure they are and were created.*
**—Revelation 4:11**

*I know that there is nothing better for them than to be glad and to get and to do good as long as they live; And also that every man should eat and drink and enjoy the good of all his labor—it is the gift of God.*
**—Ecclesiastes 3:12-13** AMP

*He has made everything beautiful in its time, he also has planted eternity in men's hearts and minds [a divinely implanted sense of a purpose working through the ages which nothing under the sun but God alone can satisfy], yet so that men cannot find out what God has done from the beginning to the end.*    **—Ecclesiastes 3:11** AMP

*Proclaim ye this among the Gentiles; Prepare war, wake up the mighty men, Let all men of war draw near; let them come up: Beat your plowshares into swords, And your pruninghooks into spears: Let the weak say, I am strong.*    **—Joel 3:9-10**

*Beloved, believe not every spirit, but try the spirits whether they are of God: because many false prophets are gone out into the world.*
**—1 John 4:1**

# THE TRIUMPH CAN'T BE HAD WITHOUT THE STRUGGLE.

*Wilma Rudolph*

# WHERE IS THE SUN?

*He made darkness His secret hiding place; as His pavilion (His canopy) round about Him were dark waters and thick clouds of the skies.*
*—Psalm 18:11* AMP

When you cannot see the light in your situation or circumstance, it is time for you to go into the secret place. Shift and move to another place in God. It is dark in the secret place and you cannot see the sun. Although God will never leave us nor forsake us, sometimes we feel like He is not there. When you *feel* like you are unable to bear the burden that you carry, you are being ushered into the secret place of God, and the sun has been darkened.

When the enemy comes in like a flood, you must remind yourself that you will triumph. When the demands seem unreasonable and you are at your wit's end, everything looks dark and gloomy. When a crisis arrives and it appears you have no control over the situation and the pitfalls and potholes seem unavoidable, you wonder where the sun is. Temporary setbacks always create opportunities for fresh commitments and renewal. When you have asked and prayed for God to elevate you to a higher level, He hides you in His shadow where it is dark. In the shadow of His wings, in the shadow of His hand, He talks to you there in the thick cloud that is round about Him. When it begins to get cloudy, you must look for the prophecy of another dimension. Do not faint. Be strong and stand in the day of adversity. We naturally want to say, "Oh Lord, let this cup pass by me." But we must remember the second part of this Scripture. Jesus said, "Nevertheless, not my will, but Your will be done."

The Spirit of Truth also hovers over the dark waters, meaning that the truth of what God has promised to do in your life will be brooding over you while you are in this dark, secret place where the devil cannot get you. The enemy will try to deceive you into thinking its all over, until God reveals He is still there by saying, "Let there be light."

After you have come through a great void and great turmoil, God will say, "Let there be light," and you will see a ray of sunshine and begin to feel the refreshing power of God. When in the beginning God created the heaven and earth, it was so.

At the next point God makes, He tells us that the earth was without form and void. God was getting ready to recreate the earth. That is what God does with us, He recreates us, and remember, we are made of the earth. God then says that darkness was upon the face of the deep. When you are in the secret place, it is dark and dismal on the surface of your deep being. While you are in this dark place, the Holy Spirit of God moves you into another dimension or realm. The New Living Translation says , "The Spirit of God was hovering over the surface of the waters"—the deep waters. Once this takes place, God will say, "Let there be light."

*For God Who said, Let light shine out of darkness, has shone in our hearts so as [to beam forth] the Light for the illumination of the knowledge of the majesty and glory of God [as it is manifest in the Person and is revealed] in the face of Jesus Christ (the Messiah). However, we possess this precious treasure [the divine Light of the Gospel] in [frail, human] vessels of earth, that the grandeur and exceeding greatness of the power may be shown to be from God and not from ourselves.*
                                         *—2 Corinthians 4:6-7* AMP

Even in the face of a divine pause, God is in control. He is working out His plan for you. Never lose hope. The sun is going to shine again. Once God has said, "Let there be light," you will know that all is good, and God will began to divide the light from darkness.

During the dark stage of process, a metamorphosis takes place in your spirit. Now that God has said, "Let there be light," He will start dividing and separating things in your life. He will begin gathering people to you that will facilitate your next assignment. I like the caterpillar illustration where we see that the struggle comes first, and then it sprouts wings and flies as a butterfly in the sun.

Whenever God is about to perform a miracle in your life, there will be opposition and persecution, which is why it gets so dark for you. Satan's goal is to abort God's Will in your life, and he will use other people to accomplish his purpose. He will use those who are in close proximity to you, those who have your ear, and those who are close to your heart. He will even use your family, those living in your home, to persecute and discourage you. Take heart, God knows your spiritual potential and He knows your limits. He will not allow you to experience adversity any longer than necessary to fulfill His purpose for you. What a comfort it is to know that God never allows us to be overloaded with tests and trials. He knows just how much we can bear.

*No weapon that is formed against thee shall prosper; and every tongue that shall rise against thee in judgment thou shalt condemn. This is the heritage of the servants of the* Lord, *and their righteousness is of me, saith the* Lord.                                      **—Isaiah 54:17**

## Overflow Scripture Meditations

*The light from the sun was gone- and suddenly the thick veil hanging in the Temple split apart.*                         **—Luke 23:45** TLB

ONLY AS HIGH AS I REACH
CAN I GROW, ONLY AS FAR AS I
SEEK CAN I GO, ONLY AS DEEP
AS I LOOK CAN I SEE, ONLY AS
MUCH AS I DREAM CAN I BE.

*Karen Ravn*

# HOPE

*May the God of hope fill you with all joy and peace as you trust in Him,*
*so that you may overflow with hope by the power of the Holy Spirit.*
*—Romans 15:13* NIV

Hope comes from God. When you trust Him with your life, He will fill you with joy and peace. You must keep on believing, expecting, and declaring the promises and the victory. Don't give up! When you absolutely feel like giving up, that is when you press in harder and declare His promises all the louder as this will empower you to overflow with hope.

As I lay there helpless, I kept on hoping to get well soon. Hope deferred makes the heart sick, so every time I felt hopeless, I would ask God to give me hope, and hope showed up. Hope is what kept me going and hope will keep you going too. Hope saves you and helps you keep your composure while you wait to see what the Spirit will do. The Bible tells us that the Spirit of God works with the hope of God to get you through anything and everything.

*For in [this] hope we were saved. But hope [the object of] which is seen is not hope. For how can one hope for what he already sees? But if we hope for what is still unseen by us, we wait for it with patience and composure. So too the [Holy] Spirit comes to our aid and bears us up in our weakness; for we do not know what prayer to offer nor how to offer it worthily as we ought, but the Spirit Himself goes to meet our supplication and pleads on our behalf with unspeakable yearnings and groanings too deep for utterance. And He Who searches the hearts of men knows what is in the mind of the [Holy] Spirit [what His intent is], because the Spirit intercedes and pleads [before God] in behalf of the saints according to and in harmony with God's will.*
*—Romans 8:24-27* AMP

It is comforting to know that the Holy Spirit is there to help us with prayers at a time when we are at our weakest. He pleads for us, yearns for us, and groans on our behalf. So when you are lying in a sick bed and all you can do is moan and groan, find peace in knowing that even with that the Spirit can make intercession for you.

*My soul, wait only upon God and silently submit to Him; for my hope and expectation are from Him.*     **—Psalm 62:5** AMP

Resting in hope is resting in God. Our God is the God of hope. You have to tell your soul to find rest, because it will not look for it automatically. The mind likes to worry and the emotions like to be on a roller-coaster. You must command your mind to be quiet, to relax, and ask God for help with your emotions; if you don't, these can put you in a pit of despair. However, if you stay hopeful and keep your mind on good thoughts, you will become a prisoner of a different sort; "a prisoner of hope." There is a remedy and a promise attached to this hope. The Bible tells us to turn to the blood of Jesus when we find ourselves in a pit.

The pit could be anything: nightmares, depression, oppression, suppression, illness, poverty, headaches, etc.—Whatever holds you down and in bondage is a dry pit without water.

*As for thee also, by the blood of thy covenant I have sent forth thy prisoners out of the pit wherein there is no water. Turn you to the strong hold, ye prisoners of hope: even today do declare that I will render double unto thee.*     **—Zechariah 9:1-12**

God will give you double when you turn to Jesus with hope. You can also remind God of His Word by saying "you said in Your Word that I shall be . . ." and fill in whatever you need for that hour, moment, or day.

*Remember your promise to me, it is my only hope. Your promise revives me; it comforts me in all my troubles.*      —*Psalm 119:49 -50* NLT

Hope is future tense and has faith looking at the promises of Almighty God, knowing with absolute assurance! Hope is the anchor of the soul. It holds you in place so that you don't drift too far away. Like I said earlier, hope deferred makes the heart sick, and this is a type of drifting away that your mind, will, and emotions will do; but even as you drift in your soul, hope, which anchors the soul, will keep you and hold you steady. Your hope will then go to the *Holy of Holies* behind the veil.

*This certain hope of being saved is a strong and trustworthy anchor for our souls, connecting us with God himself behind the sacred curtains of heaven.*      —*Hebrews 6:19* TLB

When you are sad and depressed, start praising God. Think back to the times when you sang unto the Lord with joy and gladness. Thinking back to a happier time when you sang with joy will override your emotions and allow you to sing while you are going through a difficult time. Ask yourself, "Why am I not waiting with expectation?" To change the look of despair that is on your face, start praising the Lord, it helps. Create an atmosphere of praise by shouting, singing, speaking, lifting up your hands, clapping, playing a musical instrument, dancing, bowing, and/or laying prostrate on the floor before God.

*Why art thou cast down, O my soul? And why art thou disquieted in me? Hope thou in God: for I shall yet praise him for the help of his countenance.*      —*Psalm 42:5*

God has big plans for you, and He will not let you down. It takes a lot of courage to be who you really are, especially when you cannot see who God says you are. Do not let the world tell you what that is. You must maintain hope until the end.

*For I know the plans I have for you, declares the Lord, plans to prosper you and not to harm you, plans to give you hope and a future.*
*—Jeremiah 29:11* NIV

Sing, dance, wait and pray. As you do these things, you are telling God that you are joyfully hoping for a miracle, a healing, a deliverance and so on.

*Be joyful in hope, patient in affliction, and faithful in prayer.*
*—Romans 12:12* NIV

The hope of salvation will protect you from negative thoughts that bombard your mind. Cast down vain imaginations by throwing them out. Serve an eviction notice on every high thought that tries to lift itself up and over the word of God's promises. The scripture tells us that we can wear hope as a helmet. A helmet protects your head from injury. Negative words are injurious to your mind and God has an answer to that.

*Put on the hope of salvation as a helmet.* *—1 Thessalonians 5:8* NIV

Hope also is glorious, which means; splendid, pleasant or famed. So therefore, fix yourself up, put on your best smile, allow God to get the glory of how well you look physically. Get dressed up in the name of hope. Allow your self to tap into the mystery of God by taking action in looking hopeful.

*To them God has chosen to make known among the Gentiles the glorious*

*riches of this mystery, which is Christ in you, the hope of glory.*
—*Colossians 1:27* NIV

Are you being tried? Do you know that you have been chosen to work with God? Contradicting circumstances are letting you know that now is the time to have hope, faith, and confidence

*Now faith is being sure of what we hope for and certain of what we do not see.* —*Hebrews 11:1* NIV

This book is about standing to the end, not giving up ever. Once you have hope, you must see it to the end. Faith is being sure of something that is invisible to the naked eye. Love and loving is a hope connector. Loving God and loving others by serving and ministering is a sure way to the end of hope and the beginning of faith.

*For God is not unfair. He will not forget how hard you have worked for Him and how you have shown your love to Him by caring for other Christians, as you still do. Our great desire is that you will keep right on loving others as long as life lasts, in order to make sure that what you hope for will come true.* —*Hebrews 6:11 10-11* NLT

Now when you are afflicted, comfort barely comes to mind. Yes I was sick and in bed with the pillows just right, however, I was feeling very uncomfortable about being sick, and uncomfortable about when will it be over. But Paul says that:

*Blessed be the God and Father of our Lord Jesus Christ, the Father of sympathy (pity and mercy) and the God of every comfort. Who comforts (consoles and encourages) us in every trouble (calamity and affliction), so that we may also be able to comfort those who are in any kind of trouble or distress, with the comfort with which we ourselves are comforted by God.* —*2 Corinthians 1:3-4* AMP

So now, you see that this is not just about me or just about you, rather this is for the body of Christ a well. The purpose of trouble is seen here in this passage of scripture.

*We are assured and know that all things work together and are for good to and for those who love God and are called according to His design and purpose.* —**Romans 8:28** AMP

His grace is sufficient and His strength is made perfect in my weakness and in your weakness. The Bible tells us that God delivers us from all our afflictions. He also tells us that we will learn of Him. The Lord will sustain and preserve you in your integrity (the ability to stay in faith). We are constantly reminded not to fear because God knows that the feeling of fear will come.

*Fear not [there is nothing to fear], for I am with you; do not look around you in terror and be dismayed, for I am your God. I will strengthen and harden you to difficulties, yes, I will help you; I will hold you up and retain you with My [victorious] right hand of rightness and justice.* —**Isaiah 41:10** AMP

*Many are the afflictions of the righteous: but the lord delivereth him out of them all.* —**Psalm 34:19**

### Overflow Scripture Meditations

*There is surely a future hope for you, and your hope will not be cut off.* —**Proverbs 23:18** NIV

*My rightness and justice are near, My salvation is going forth, and My arms shall rule the peoples; the islands shall wait for and expect Me, and on My arm shall they trust and wait with hope.* —**Isaiah 51:5** AMP

*Through Him also we have access (entrance, introduction) by faith into this grace in which we firmly and safely stand. And let us rejoice and exult in our hope of experiencing and enjoying the glory of God.*

*—Romans 5:2* AMP

DO NOT CARRY ANYTHING INTO
YOUR NEW FUTURE OTHER THAN
THE LESSONS YOU LEARNED AND
THE TESTIMONIES GOD GIVES YOU.

*Creflo Dollar*

# STANDING IN FAITH

*Now faith is the substance of things hoped for, the evidence of things not seen.*                                    *—Hebrews 11:1*

Unlike hope, which is future tense, faith is present tense. And it is a free gift that grows out of the Word of God. Faith is proof-positive assurance that the thing you have fondly hoped for is at last yours for the taking.

God allows trouble so that He may teach you His Word and how to work His Word. It is impossible to please God without His Word. Before anything else existed, the Word was there with God. This Word is Christ Himself. To go a little further, we know that Christ is the author of our faith, meaning the beginning of our faith. This tells me that Jesus is the Word and the Word is the beginning of our faith. This Word is our faith and therefore to please God, we must have Jesus who is also the finisher of our faith. Standing in and on faith means trusting and leaning on Jesus, the Word made flesh. (See John 1:1-3.) Jesus is faith personified. His name is Faithful, Wonderful, Counselor, and the Mighty Prince.

*Looking unto Jesus the author and finisher of our faith; who for the joy that was set before Him endured the cross, despising the shame, and is set down at the right hand of the throne of God.*                    *—Hebrews 12:2*

A measure of faith has been given to each of us. You first received a measure of faith for salvation. Now if you want miracles, healing, and deliverance, you will need another measure of faith. At first you cannot see your healing, or the miracle, or the deliverance, so you get into the Word to receive a measure of faith. Remember, faith is the substance of things hoped for. You are hoping for healing, deliverance, and a miracle. Getting into faith requires getting into the Word. The Word of God is the substance of things hoped for and it has been proven that it brings forth what you cannot see. Standing on the Word is standing on your faith in Jesus.

*And straightway the father of the child cried out, and said with tears, Lord, I believe; help thou mine unbelief.* —**Mark 9:24**

When you ask God to increase your faith and you know that faith comes from the Word, than you should increase your Word. The Word comes by hearing and hearing and hearing. Search out every Scripture pertaining to what you are going through and do not let the fear of what you are going through contaminate your faith. Fear is an enemy of faith. Fear does not come from God. Fear tells you God won't do what He said He will do. God says heaven and earth will pass away, but My Word shall forever stand. (See Matthew 24:35.) That is why I am telling you to stand on the Word of God.

*For in Jesus Christ neither circumcision availeth any thing, nor uncircumcision; but faith which worketh by love.* —**Galatians 5:6**

Do not get caught up in how you Feel. Feelings do not dictate what God is doing in your life. Emotions change from moment to moment and are not needed in our faith. Your spirit locks the Word in, locks the faith in, and says "it is so" and "it shall be done." So even when your feelings don't tell you God is going to do it, the Word shall forever stand.

No one will be able to say to you, "The Word doesn't work." No one will have to convince you that the Word works. You will say, "I tried it and it worked!" The more of the Word you get, the more faith you've got! If you got a little faith for God to do something, start searching the scriptures diligently so that you will have a lot of Word which leads to a lot of faith. Ask, knock, and seek! Eat the bread, and drink the water, and then out of your belly shall flow living faith.

The Bible tells us that faith without works is dead and almost every believer has heard that Scripture, however, not many actually realize that work means taking action. One of the best actions to take is the action of prayer. Prayer works and your work is to pray. Working in this capacity allows God to download instruction into your spirit so that you will be equipped to stand in faith.

As you diligently obey what God tells you to do in spite of your circumstances, you will see long-suffering develop in your life. Longsuffering is patient endurance. Long-suffering is an important quality to have if you want to see the promises of God. Do not give up, cave in, or quit when you do not see the answers to your prayers right away. The predicament that you find yourself in will be fairly judged and Jesus will go to war for you. Know that if God said it, He will do it.

*After that I saw heaven opened, and behold, a white horse [appeared]! The One Who was riding it is called Faithful (Trustworthy, Loyal, Incorruptible, Steady) and True, and He passes judgment and wages war in righteousness (holiness, justice, and uprightness).*
*—Revelation 19:11* AMP

Knowing the significance of the names of Jesus gives clarity on every level. When talking about faith, it is reassuring to know that Jesus is called Faithful and True. Do not believe the lies of the devil. Everything Jesus says is faithful and true because He is Faithful and True.

*The title by which He is called is The Word of God.*
*—Revelation 19:13b* AMP

## Overflow Scripture Meditations

*That ye be not slothful, but followers of them who through faith and patience inherit the promises.*       **—Hebrews 6:12**

*For when God made promises to Abraham, because he could swear by no greater, he swore by himself.*       **—Hebrews 6:13**

*And so, after he had patiently endured, he [Abraham] obtained the promise.*       **—Hebrews 6:15**

# DISCIPLINE WEIGHS OUNCES; REGRET WEIGHS TONS.

*Author Unknown*

# BESETTING SIN

*Let no man say when he is tempted, I am tempted from God; for God is incapable of being tempted by [what is] evil and He Himself tempts no one. But every person is tempted when he is drawn away, enticed and baited by his own evil desire (lust, passions). Then the evil desire, when it has conceived, gives birth to sin, and sin, when it is fully matured, brings forth death.*                                      *—James 1:13-15* AMP

The devil will use the same tactics to get you into sin that he used on Eve in the Garden and Jesus in the wilderness. He has nothing new to come with; let us not be ignorant of his plots. There are three gates to your soul and body that provide an entryway through which the devil tempts:

1.  The lust of the flesh
2.  The lust of the eyes
3.  The pride of life

In the Garden of Eden, satan came to Eve questioning what she knew of God's authority. Eve answered incorrectly because she didn't fully understand the Word. Eve thought she would die if she touched the fruit. When that turned out to be false, satan was able to lure her into eating the fruit. Eve saw that the tree was good for food (lust of the flesh), that it was pleasant to the eyes (lust of the eyes), and that it was a tree to be desired to make one wise (pride of life).

The lust of the flesh says, "I have to have it!" It makes excuses sound like reasons. It is the preoccupation with one's appetite and satiation of urges, drives, and desires.

The lust of the eyes causes you to be materialistic. You want things that make you look wealthy and attractive. It makes you self-centered, self-seeking, and superficial. Image becomes everything.

Pride is essentially a declaration of independence from God because it produces an inordinate opinion of self and personal superiority. The spirit of pride caused satan to believe that he could be God.

After Jesus had been led into the wilderness by the Spirit of God to fast for 40 days, satan came to Him with the same tactic he came to Eve with. Temptation can only occur when it is something you want to have. Satan knew Jesus was hungry; he knew Jesus had not eaten any food for 40 days. So he began by questioning who He was in God, "Are you really the son of God? If so, command that these stones be made bread" (lust of the flesh). And he told Him, "Cast thyself down that the angels may catch you" (pride of life). Then satan took Him up an exceedingly high mountain and showed Him all the kingdoms of the earth (lust of the eyes). Jesus, however, knew the Word of God and was able to resist where Eve had faltered.

*Wherefore seeing we also are compassed about with so great a cloud of witnesses, let us lay aside every weight, and the sin which doth so easily beset us, and let us run with patience the race that is set before us.*
*—Hebrews 12:1*

Sin holds you back, wraps you up, and trips you. Like I said earlier, you may not be fully aware of what is going on with you and sin, because of its deceptive ways. The Hebrew word for *sin* is *chattath,* from the root word *chatta,* and in Greek it is *humaria.* Both words mean "to miss the mark." As it relates to God's law, they mean that one has failed to meet the standard or missed the targeted mark set by God for us. God's mark or standard is His Law. Therefore sin is the transgression of any of the laws of God. (See John 3:4.) Sin needs to be removed. Any hindrance that could be used to slow your progress needs to be set aside. (See Psalm 51.)

*Neither give place to the devil.*                 *—Ephesians 4:27*

Disobedience to God will often bring affliction in our lives. Even when we are not aware of it, our sins easily beset us. When you find yourself in a situation that causes you to sit, think, and wonder what went wrong, consider sin. As you meditate and pray, God will reveal to you what sin needs to be addressed. He will allow you a chance to come clean about it, so do not ignore the truth. If you do, you will be in disobedience. You do not want to defy and resist the authority of God, and you do not want to refuse His chastening. Failing to obey a command or direct order from God is rebellion. Pride and stubbornness is as witchcraft, idolatry, and iniquity. This is especially disheartening when it comes to chosen believers who sincerely love the Lord and want to serve Him. If you are having trouble with these things, pray for a mind renewal and ask God to establish your thoughts. We ought to always obey God. Obedience is a duty to be performed and a decision to be practiced.

*Samuel replied, "Has the Lord as much pleasure in your burnt offering and sacrifices as in your obedience? Obedience is far better than sacrifice. He is much more interested in your listening to Him than in your offering the fat of rams to him. For rebellion is as bad as the sin of witchcraft, and stubbornness is as bad as worshipping idols. And now because you have rejected the Word of Jehovah, he has rejected you from being king."*
—*1 Samuel 15:22-23* TLB

You do not want to give the devil a place to hang out in your soul. Get rid of all that is wrong in your life, both inside and outside, by acknowledging, confessing, and repenting. God will send help. Be glad for the wonderful revelation that is given to you to save your soul.

*If we say that we have no sin, we deceive ourselves, and the truth is not in us. If we confess our sins, he is faithful and just to forgive us our sins, and to cleanse us from all unrighteousness.* —*I John 1:8-9*

Do not make concessions to things that are detrimental to your spirit, soul, and mind. A compromising decision will lower the value of a biblical standard and leave you unprotected. Ask God to take away all that is not of Him and create a right spirit within you. It is the inner man that is expressed through the outer man we see when we look at each other. We want the spirit of conviction and excellence working in us at all times. Psalm 119:11 states "Your word I have hidden in my heart, that I might not sin against You.

*Let not then your good be evil spoken of.*        **—Romans 14:16**

Do not worry. Worry is an apprehensive or distressed state of mind. Jesus gives us much insight into the futility of worry, especially in light of the alternative: faith. Believe in our heavenly Father, the Provider and the Giver and Sustainer of life, to bestow peace in troubled times. Worry will change your physical and mental well-being into high blood pressure, insomnia, anxiety, weight loss, weight gain, hair loss and a host of other conditions. Worry is a mask of fear. It is meditating on a negative thing or outcome; spending time on the contradictions of what God's Word says. Paul reminds us in Philippians 4:8 to think on positive things of good report. We should think of good answers to all negative reports. Pray the answer, not the problem. Remember, don't pray if you are going to worry, and don't worry if you are going to pray.

When we become relaxed in our prayer life, and the flame in our spirit is getting low on oil, the devil finds this to be a good time to attack. You know when you get exasperated waiting for God to answer prayers and your answers are taking too long to manifest. You get lazy in Bible study, you don't spend as much time in prayer, and you start skipping out on church. Discouragement sets in, because our expectations are not met. The enemy often chooses this time to attack, because we are not built up spiritually. Our behavior shows that we are low on spiritual food which is the Word of God. We need to start singing the Juanita Bynum song, "I Don't Mind Waiting."

*Be sober, be vigilant; because your adversary the devil, as a roaring lion, walketh about, seeking whom he may devour.*      —*1 Peter 5:8*

Satan searches for your weak spots. He knows just what buttons to push and sometimes knows them better than you do. He waits until you let your guard down and strikes hard.

Another sin that easily besets us is unforgiveness: the refusal to release someone from an offense or wrong doing. Unforgiveness grieves the Holy Spirit and is sometimes one of the most difficult sins to confess and to get over because we so often think we must feel it emotionally when we forgive someone. The very act of forgiveness is an act of our will and not of our emotions. It is essential that we learn how to express true forgiveness, with open hands and open hearts, and no leftover residue of resentment. Forgiveness is the willingness to change your attitude about a strained relationship.

If unforgiveness is left to fester, it has the potential to give rise to bitterness and grudges. Characteristics of unforgiveness include anger, hurt, hatred, ill-will, and deep-seated resentment. Replaying an event or an act of vengeance keeps you in bondage to an offense. As long as an act of wrongdoing remains in your thoughts, you have not forgiven.

Forgiveness is the key that unlocks the door of resentment and the handcuffs of hate. It provides the grace to change our course in life, preventing collisions that otherwise might prove to be catastrophic. Sometimes you have to forgive yourself too. Some hurts are unforgettable, but forgiveness heals you. Forgiveness is not necessarily for the person who hurt you—it sets *you* free. You are not submitting to their brutality, injustice, or offense. Don't grieve the spirit by holding on to things too long. Cast your care on the Lord. Allow His grace to permeate your mind, soul, and emotions. Forgiving must be your immediate priority. You cannot pray effectively without forgiving.

*So if when you are offering your gift at the altar you there remember that your brother has any [grievance] against you, leave your gift at the altar and go. First make peace with your brother, and then come back and present your gift.*        **—Matthew 5:23-24** AMP

Forgiving means leaving everything in God's hands, remembering that ultimately, vengeance is His alone. Allow yourself to think differently, change your mind, and change your conduct. Repent! Repent! Repent!

*Create in me a clean heart, O God. Renew a loyal spirit within me.*        **—Psalm 51:10** NLT

Many times the Christian life seems like an endless string of adversity, trials, and assorted problems which could be confusing at times. We must be careful to check ourselves against murmuring and complaining. We have to make a decision to look on the bright side. It is easy to grumble at the gloomy side of life's troubles and become depressed. God wants us to have hope in the midst of confusion and not give in, but not only hope in this life, also hope of eternity. Find joy in this truth also.

Murmuring and complaining are not usually recognized as sin. When you are in adversity, it is easy to rationalize this type of behavior. Do not be deceived into thinking grumbling is okay because you are going through something.

I can tell you how I dealt with this problem in my own situation. I lived with other people who stayed up past my bedtime and every morning I would wake up to a dirty kitchen. This just about drove me nuts. I grumbled every morning. The devil could count on me to start my day off complaining. God does not take His children's grumbling so lightly. One day The Holy Spirit led me to hear a sermon on grumbling. From that hour I made a decision to start singing every morning as I washed dishes and cleaned the floor while everyone else slept. When the murmuring would try to rise up in me, I sang more passionately and would throw my hands up and dance on the kitchen floor.

In times past, God took stern action against grumblers. The Israelites in the wilderness got this:

*The Lord sent fiery serpents among the people, and they bit the people; and much people of Israel died.* —**Numbers 21:6**

How do you get fixed? How do you address these subtle sins? Get pruned like a fruit tree with many branches. In the church, the branches all claim to be followers of Christ. However, the fruitful branches are chosen believers who, by their walk with Christ, produce much fruit. The unproductive branches will be separated from the vine. Jesus tells us that He is the Vine and the Father is the Vine dresser who cares for the branches to make them fruitful. (See John 15:1-8.)

During the pruning process a tree often bleeds sap. The caretaker binds up the open branches so the tree will remain strong. The sap itself solidifies and acts like a bandage over the open cut. So when you are in this process, do not worry, God will send help for the open cuts and wounds you sustain.

In the Christian life, branches can be characteristic of our spiritual development in specific areas. One branch represents our love for others. One is forgiveness, one is mercy, and another is generosity. Each one of these branches must be pruned by God. As chosen believers, God will not allow sin to compromise our growth as we pray, fast, and give. When God gets ready to promote us to a higher level of living, pruning is necessary.

As the Lord began to prune me, He showed me that my family obligations had become a codependency for me. To be burdened for people and situations is expected of all saints, especially when it comes to the redemptive purpose of God being manifested. However, satan wants to put false burdens upon you that cause undue stress, pressure, and discomfort. These burdens are easily distinguishable from the authentic ones in that they are heavy, often unbearable, and do not come from God. Jesus said He would teach us how to find rest and give light burdens. It took me a long time to overcome the overwhelming burden I felt for my family.

*Take my yoke upon you, and learn of me; for I am meek and lowly in heart: and ye shall find rest unto your souls. For my yoke is easy, and my burden is light.*      **—Matthew 11:29-30**

I watched God prune one responsibility after another out of my life. He taught me how to delegate chores, duties, and responsibilities to those that were counting on me to handle everything. I was burning out and was suffering from separation anxiety just thinking about leaving. This was a psychological and emotional attachment God had to show me how to break. I was in need of interdependent relationships. I was weary and carrying heavy burdens.

*Come unto me, all ye that labor and are heavy laden and I will give you rest.*      **—Matthew 11:28**

God was showing me my future ministry, and I saw how I was to help, but I had to learn of God's way, which was a better way. What I thought was ministering to my family was not the proper method.

You need to understand that God is always trying to tell you something about your life and situation. Below is a passage from a book I frequently read:

[Not all casualties of war are caused by the enemy, but sometimes by those closest to us. This is not to imply that they have malicious intent, that they are motivated to destroy us, or intentionally harm us. But they can be used by the enemy to accidently hurt or destroy us in spite of their sincere love for us. One of the reasons why this weapon is so powerful is that the actual weapons used are their love and positive regard, rather than their hatred or ill will toward us.]

Getting back to the analogy of the trees: there is a season in the life of certain maple trees when men collect sap from them. During the proper season, we obtain a sweet wonderful addition to pancakes, waffles, and biscuits. But out of season, it is bitter and tasteless. So happy is the man whose sap is sweetened by adversity and the standing on the Word of God. Remember that there is a season for every activity under heaven.

*And it shall come to pass in that day, that his burden shall be taken away from off thy shoulder, and his yoke from off thy neck, and the yoke shall be destroyed because of the anointing.*     —*Isaiah 10:27*

The bonsai tree is small and beautiful to look at . As it is pruned or cut back, it reaches out farther. I say this to inform you that when God prunes you, your branches will eventually reach out farther than before and you will be able to reach more people. Your territory becomes larger and the prayer of Jabez is answered.

*"Oh that You would bless me indeed, and enlarge my territory, that Your hand would be with me, and that You would keep me from evil, that I may not cause pain!" So God granted him what he requested.*     —*1 Chronicles 4:10* NKJV

Fruit trees are pruned to remain small enough for the fruit to be picked. Jesus wants us to be fruitful and multiply, so God will continue to prune our lives so that the people we are ministering to may reach and pick the spiritual fruit we produce.

It is difficult to leave behind the familiar past, the besetting sin and comfort zone, and venture into new territory. So we cling to ideas, habits, and people that we should let go of. God knows about the things in our lives that need to be cut away, and when we are honest with ourselves, we know too.

*This is my comfort in my affliction: For thy word hath quickened me.*
                                                        —**Psalm 119:50**

The way we walk always identifies our purpose. You can usually tell where a person has been or where they are going by looking at how they walk. As a believer, do not listen and walk according to worldly views, ideas, advice, habits and opinions. These things easily beset in us because we are in the world. Please remember that although we are in the world, we are no longer of the world. When your walk displays ungodly attributes, you actually reflect these things to others. This why the pruning process is necessary. You are truly blessed when your body reflects the character of God. You walk with your body. Your body is the temple that carries the Holy Spirit.

Your soul includes your mind, will, emotions, and intellect. You do not want to sin by rationalizing that everything's perfect with you, but less than perfect with others. You must guard your soul to ensure it doesn't get lifted up because you've grown so much in God, and then find fault with everybody else. You can always look around to see somebody who is "lower" than you, struggling with something you have already overcome. Do not put people down. Be careful not to stand in the way of a sinner and their salvation with your haughty behavior or pride. Do not assume all is right with you just because God is using you. Remember, a man's gift makes room for him, and brings him before great men. (See Proverbs 18:16), but pride goes before destruction, and a haughty spirit before a fall (see Proverbs 16:18).

Your spirit sits in your loins. Your loins are used for walking, standing, and sitting. As we walk in the Spirit, we should not follow the advice of evil men. I stated earlier that the way we walk always identifies our purpose. Upright purpose to walk uprightly. You also do not want to sit down with sinners scoffing at the things of God. Stay away from toxic people and toxic situations. Love them from a distance. Stand firm in mercy and grace.

*Blessed is the man who walks not in the counsel of the ungodly, nor standeth in the way of sinners, nor sitteth in the seat of the scornful. But his delight is in the delight of the LORD; and in his law doth he meditate day and night. And he shall be like a tree planted by the rivers of water, that bringeth forth in his season; his leaf shall not wither; and whatsoever he doeth shall prosper.*      **—Psalm 1:1-3**

Step by step, we walk in the Word. Jesus is the Word, and Jesus is the Light, which means we walk in the Light. And no matter how many times we miss the Christian mark, the blood will cover it. Walking in the light allows you to go to God in truth through acknowledgment and confession. (See Psalm 32:5.) Do not hesitate to ask God for an escape when temptation comes your way. When pressure is applied to your flesh to act or speak in an ungodly way, God can and will get you out of it.

*The Lord knoweth how to deliver the godly out of temptations.*      **—2 Peter 2:9a**

God will send notice to help you prepare for His coming, for He will come to process you through purification. (See Malachi 3:1-3; 16-18; and Hebrews 12:28.) In 1 John 3:8, John wrote that Jesus purpose was to destroy the works of the devil. God sent Jesus to die for the price of our sins. Jesus bore our sin and the guilty condemnation that accompanies it. Once God breaks the yoke of sin from us, He removes the guilt too. Condemnation differs from conviction. The Holy Spirit sets off the alarm of conviction in our conscience so we can recognize sin, but not condemnation. The power of the blood of Jesus continuously cleanses us. This process is called conviction and it is of the Lord, while condemnation is from the enemy. If we heed conviction, it will lift us up and out of sin; condemnation only makes you feel bad about yourself and takes away your confidence in God's mercy and grace.

## Overflow Scripture Meditations

*Wherefore lay apart all filthiness and superfluity of naughtiness, and receive with meekness the engrafted word, which is able to save your souls.*                                                    —*James 1:21*

*If we who are [abiding] in Christ have hope only in this life and that is all, then we are of all people most miserable and to be pitied.*
                                             —*1 Corinthians 15:19* AMP

*But if we walk in the light, as he is in the light, we have fellowship one with another, and the blood of Jesus Christ his Son cleanseth us from all sin.*                                                     —*1 John 1:7*

*Then Peter and the other apostles answered and said, We ought to obey God rather than men.*                                      —*Acts 5:29*

*And they departed from the presence of the council, rejoicing that they were counted worthy to suffer shame for his name.*     **—Acts 5:41**

*There is a way which seems right to a man and appears straight before him, but at the end of it is the way of death.*    **—Proverbs 14:12** AMP

*Have mercy and be gracious unto me, O Lord, for I am in trouble; with grief my eye is weakened, also my inner self and my body.*

**—Psalm 31:9**

THERE ARE GOING TO BE
DISAPPOINTMENTS, BUT WE
CAN RISE ABOVE THEM.

*Hope Fisher*

# UNSOUND AND UNSTABLE

*Blessed (happy, fortunate, to be envied) is the man whose strength is in You, in whose heart are the highways to Zion. Passing through the Valley of Weeping (Baca), they make it a place of springs; the early rain also fills [the pools] with blessings.* —*Psalm 84:5-6* AMP

The Valley of Baca, also known as the valley of Weeping, is a place where your soul is weak and your strength is low. A valley by definition is a depression between peaks. Another definition is an elongated lowland between ranges of mountains, hills, or other uplands. Weeping can occur from loss, injury, death of a loved one, betrayal, frustration, abandonment, fear, debt, poverty, sickness, fatigue, or disobedience to name a few.

According to the Scripture above, the valleys of weeping can be turned into springs. Writing this chapter was difficult for me because I was reminded of how painful pain is. Whatever the mountain of pain is, weeping is the antidote. When the tears will not stop, find comfort and strength in the Scripture above.

God sees your heart and knows that you are on the highway to Zion. He knows that you are only passing through this valley. Every now and then you encounter the kind of pain that will leave you in a low or depressed place, and you don't know how long this valley is. Sometimes, an emotional earthquake causes us to be shaken to pieces and we are left with a pool of tears. These tears are falling down like rain and are creating pools that God has promised to fill with blessings. The early rain signifies the tears coming before the blessing, before the breakthrough, and before the joy. Just as rain cleans the air, our tears cleanses the pressure from the soul and spirit. So let the tears fall because God can and God will heal you of your heart of disappointment. Let the promise of blessings give you hope and help you to believe and to trust again. You will not stay in this valley forever, even though, for the moment, it may seem like there is no healing good enough to ease or erase the pain. I had to learn through experience how to search for beauty and meaning in the emptiness, the loneliness, and the sadness that come with weeping and mourning.

Loneliness is one of our greatest fears and most intense emotional pains. This is a mountain that could place you in the valley of Baca. The enemy wants us to believe that we are alone, unwanted, unworthy, and unloved. But Jesus came to let every person know that they are loved, valued, and never alone. So as the tears fall, God will fill your pools with the blessing of His love.

I have included some definitions for the words *unsound* and *unstable* to help you identify several meanings.

"Unsound: not dependably strong or solid; not physically or mentally healthy; not true or logically valid; not whole; not wholly sane; disordered; impaired."

"Unstable: irregular; wavering in purpose; liable to fall or sway; lacking control of one's emotions; unpredictable behavior; not firm or fixed."

The most precious commodity in the earth realm is the mind. The enemy works against us through our thoughts. Many unhealthy thoughts bombard our mind when we have been in an emotional fight. Spiritual warfare, in its purest form, is the council of the human mind by any spirit other than the spirit of the Lord. You must try every spirit by the Spirit of God. Deliberate deception and manipulation are used to defeat us. Little nagging thoughts, fears, wonderings, and theories bombard our minds. The enemy wants us to think these are our own thoughts. Fight against the thoughts by speaking the promises God gives in His Word out loud. You must talk back to the enemy with what is written in God's Word.

Physical and verbal abuse will leave you mentally unsound and emotionally unstable. You must cry out to God the loudest and the strongest from your valley. A major deliverance is required and you must draw your strength from God. As you do, you will find yourself going "from strength to strength" and "increasing in victorious power," as Psalm 84:7 promises. In time you will discover that the wisdom of God will reveal the intent and content of a person's heart, so that you will recognize insincere people around you. If you have ever been brainwashed to think you are inferior in any type of way, the effects can be long lasting. This is a great struggle. Remember that you are just passing through the Valley of Baca. Observe what the enemy is doing and saying then pray the opposite.

The death of a loved one is devastating to the emotions. Since there is a time to live and a time to die, you may have to return to this valley many times. There are a lot of hurting people unable to find their way out. This valley reminds me of a movie I saw years ago entitled What Dreams May Come, where after the death of two children and a husband, the wife commits suicide. The husband, being in a good place, decided to go into the place of suicides to bring his wife out. She was stuck in a pit of despair, and he needed a guide to take him to where she was. It is just this kind of pit that God wants to deliver you from and will fill with blessings. Help is on the way. The Holy Spirit is our guide and He will lead us into all truth. You cannot lead someone else on a path that you yourself have not traveled. I have been in the Valley of Baca and I know the way out.

When we are tired, lonely, and weighing big decisions the enemy will try to tap into the weak spots of our minds. During the times that we are the most vulnerable, the most frustrated, during our lowest of lows when we cannot see our way out or when we are devastated, our world becomes chaotic. Things and people get on your nerves and your reserve nerves. You can't find anyone who understands what you are going through and the temptation to give up comes in a lot of ways.

*Though, now for a season, if need be, ye are in heaviness through manifold temptations.*        *—1 Peter 1:6*

When you are going through hell, don't stop—keep walking, keep going, because on the other side of your faith and obedience are the miracle and the breakthrough that you have been praying and believing God for.

Mental and emotional trauma caused by the pain of betrayal from a spouse will leave you feeling unsound and unstable. This will produce a cry from the depths of your soul. A weeping of the soul begins when you don't know what to pray. The tears are crying out to God. This is not just a broken heart, this is a broken soul that is crying out like a woman in labor. Betrayal is hurtful and unexpected, causing you great anger and disappointment. God tells us to make it a place of springs. A spring is a flow of water, and for you, dear chosen one, it is a flow of tears. He says the rain—the tears—will fill the pools. A pool is an accumulation of liquid—a small body of water. So start digging for a well when you find yourself in this place. A well has water in it, and the valley of Baca is a dry place. God tells us to dig because He knows that there is thirst-quenching spiritual water to be found deep down in our souls. Living water runs deep. Digging into God's Word is digging a well for the living water. Your digging will strengthen your spiritual muscles.

Every struggle has an ending. Say to yourself "This is the greatest attack I've ever had, but I know that on the other side is the greatest victory I've ever had!"

*Falling down ain't falling down if you don't cry when you hit the floor.*
                                                              *Alicia Keys*

*For God hath not given us the spirit of fear; but of power, and of love,
and of a sound mind.*                                      **—2 Timothy 1:7**

While in prayer you ask God to heal your bitterness, sadness, anger, rage, and pain. Empowerment comes from God. The Holy Spirit will teach you how to be able to discern the spirit, intents, and motives of those operating around and interacting with you. Deal with prolonged emotional pain by seeking God's face continually.

Jesus did not depend on His human feelings. He had them, but He knew not to lean on them. Feelings do not always tell the truth or agree with God's Word.

The Bible also tells us not to lean on our own understanding. Emotions change, and our understanding is not full enough. Achieving victory requires discipline. All thoughts are not qualified to legitimately be in your mind. (See Philippians 4:8.) If your thoughts are not true, honest, just, pure, lovely, of good report, or praiseworthy, do not allow them to take root in your mind. Demolish, annihilate, and conquer these thoughts by casting them down. Make sure you repent of any and every thing you have done or thought that misses the high mark of Christ's calling for your life.

*For it was not an enemy that reproached me; then I could have borne
it: neither was it he that hated me that did magnify himself against me;
then I would have his myself from him: but it was thou, a man mine
equal, my guide, and acquaintance. We took sweet counsel together, and
walked unto the house of God in company.*          **—Psalm 55:12-14**

Abandonment can raise havoc with your emotional and mental state whether it come from a relative, a friend, or a spouse. When a person withdraws his/her presence and support from you; or reneges on his/her duty, responsibility, and obligation; or betrays trust, covenant, or commitment; you typically are thrust into great emotional pain, financial hardship, and/or spiritual misalignment. You must be careful not to take on the role of victim. Do not give your personal power away. The emotional pain of abandonment hurts like hell, leaving you in a state of confusion. When a person violates a promise, whether verbal or written, it robs one of trust and causes intense grief to the soul. It leaves you in a state of chaos and with a fear of rejection you cannot easily shake off. You become suspicious, lonely, and feel ashamed. But remember! You are just passing through.

A parent dies, leaving us feeling unanchored; a spouse walks out, tearing up our emotions, we feel unsound. A job is gone—where is the security? Through all of this, we must make a decision to survive. How you get through this will be determined by your degree of preparedness, your knowledge of what is taking place, your psychological outlook, your mental and emotional stability, and those who stand ready to help you.

Changes occur that we may not be ready to embrace. As we age and go through the stages of life, our minds and emotions try to make sense of being human. For sisters, we keep getting hot and sweaty even while we sleep. We have mood swings with little to no warning. We go through psychological changes and feel unstable. The brothers start losing their hair, their teeth began to disappear, bones start aching more often, and that all-pregnant look shows up.

As we grow older, we go through a spiritual change as well as a natural change. Even though our outward man is perishing, our inward man is renewed day-by-day. We pass from death unto life. We become a new creature in Christ Jesus.

*The Lord God hath given me the tongue of the learned, That I should know how to speak a word in season to him that is weary.*

*—Isaiah 50:4*

I have touched on several topics that are designed to take over your mind. This is where the battle is. When there is a storm happening in your life, do what Jesus did and declare, "Peace, be still! Continuing in His Word is how you will stay victorious over all the lies of the devil. The Word is truth and the truth shall make you free from mental and emotional bondage.

*Finally, my brethren, be strong in the Lord, and in the power of His might. Put on the whole armor of God, that ye may be able to stand against the wiles of the devil.*          *—Ephesians 6:10-11*

A wile is a stronghold of your mind. The devil wants to keep a stronghold on your mind, rendering you unstable and unsound. A stronghold is a thought pattern, a mindset, and mental processes that cause you to act, react, and respond in a particular manner. When you are hurt and weeping, remember that there is a time to cry. The Scriptures tells us that weeping may endure for the night (season), but joy comes in the morning. Remember, there is also a time to laugh. Getting stuck in grief is suicide. Do not respond contrary to the ways of God and rationalize to justify your behavior. Satan uses this to set up strongholds in your mind. The Bible tells us that we are not to be ignorant of the devils devices, which is why I am telling you this right now. Do not be stubborn and continue to blame your behavior on how you were raised, or "this is our tradition." We must continually put on the helmet of salvation to protect our minds.

*For we wrestle not against flesh and blood, but against principalities, against powers, against the rulers of the darkness of this world, against spiritual wickedness in high places.*          *—Ephesians 6:12*

## Overflow Scriptures Meditations

*And when he came to himself, he said, How many hired servants of my father's have bread enough and to spare, and I perish with hunger!*
                                      **—Luke 15:17**

*My heart is sore pained within me: and the terrors of death are fallen upon me. Fearfulness and trembling are come upon me, and horror hath overwhelmed me. And I said, Oh that I had wings like a dove! For then I would fly away, and be at rest.*          **—Psalm 55:4-6**

*Finally, brethren, whatsoever things are true, whatsoever things are honest, whatsoever things are just, whatsoever things are pure, whatsoever things are lovely, whatsoever things are of good report; if there be any virtue, and if there be any praise, think on these things.*
                                     **—Philippians 4:8**

*(For the weapons of our warfare are not carnal, but mighty through God to the pulling down of strong holds;) Casting down imaginations, and every high thing that exhalteth itself against the knowledge of God, and bringing into captivity every thought to the obedience of Christ.*
                                  **—2 Corinthians 10:4-5**

*Therefore they shall come and sing in the height of Zion, and shall flow together to the goodness of the Lord... and their soul shall be as a watered garden; and they shall not sorrow any more at all.*
                                  **—Jeremiah 31:12**

*Then said Jesus to those Jews which believed on him, If ye continue in my word, then are ye my disciples indeed; and ye shall know the truth, and the truth shall make you free.*         **—John 8:31-32**

WHEN THE DEVIL CANNOT
GET YOUR SPIRIT, HE WILL
ATTACK YOU IN YOUR BODY.

*T. D. Jakes*

# SICK AND TIRED

*When Jesus received the message, He said, This sickness is not to end in death; but [on the contrary] it is to honor God and to promote His glory, that the Son of God may be glorified through (by) it.*

*—John 11:4* AMP

When you are sick, your body is weak. If you endure weakness for too long, you become very tired of being sick. The mind has plenty of time to think about never getting well, staying sick for the rest of your life, and death itself. Illness is like a dark, haunting, hopeless valley. You feel like you are all alone. The days and nights become a blur. During my sickness, I kept reminding myself that God was doing a great work in me, because I felt so weak and the Bible tells us that God is strongest when we are weakest. So I stood on that Word with all I had. God seemed to be very quiet. He was not speaking to me audibly and things were standing still in my life. This is a time when satan will try to deceive you into thinking God does not care or that your time has come and you are going to die. Satan talks to your mind and challenges your identity. You have to be patient and wait on God's still small voice. In the Bible, we are told to wait on the Lord and He shall give us strength, answers, and instructions.

Looking at the story of Job reminds us of how subtle deception can be. It can come through well-meaning people who hurry to analyze your situation. They seem to know more about you than you do yourself. Sometimes you must turn a deaf ear to everyone. So, it is your personal responsibility to learn to know God's voice for yourself. That way if the whole world tells you one thing and God tells you something else, you will have the strength and the boldness to follow God. God's Word is a ready weapon, like a two-edged sword. This sword will jump up in your hand when you need it to fight against the lies of the devil. Even though our outward man is perishing, our inward man is renewed day-by-day.

*For the word of God is quick, and powerful, and sharper than any two-edged sword, piercing even to the dividing asunder of soul and spirit, and of the joints and marrow, and is a discerner of the thoughts and intents of the heart.*     **—Hebrews 4:12**

I want you to notice the words "joints and marrow." These are related to your physical body. When the devil is telling you lies about your sickness and tries to keep your thoughts in a negative realm, speak hope filled words that prevail over his words. Words like "I am healed," and "By His stripes I am healed." The Word is able to discern truth from lie for you. The soul is your mind, will, and emotions, and when you are sick, all three are under attack. You must know God's Word on healing and health; you must know God's promises for healing and health.

*The Lord will strengthen him upon his bed of languishing: Thou wilt make all his bed in his sickness.*     **—Psalm 41:3**

You do not have to listen and heed to the negative report about your health. Even when the report comes from well-meaning people, ask of the Lord, and He will give you help. Yes, we tend to want to rely on our own understanding, but God is in control and He wants you to know it.

*Thou through thy commandments hast made me wiser than mine enemies.*     **—Psalm 119:98**

Sickness is suffering. Suffering for Jesus's sake will be worth it. Jesus is in the business of restoration. He will restore your health. According to Mark 3:1-5, Jesus restored the hand of a man on the Sabbath day which by law was illegal. There are a lot of reasons why you shouldn't get restoration according to the law. However, since Jesus has stepped on the scene, we have been given grace: the unmerited favor of God.

*Indeed, we felt within ourselves that we received the [very] sentence of death, but that was to keep us from trusting in and depending on ourselves instead of on God Who raises the dead.*
                                    *—2 Corinthians 1:9* AMP

Your job is to stand in faith for your healing and health. And having done all to stand, stand therefore till the end of your salvation. Fight for your healing and health. In the following Scripture, Paul reminds us of the future times of affliction we shall face, because many are the afflictions of the righteous. Righteous, right living, and living to please God places you in a position to be afflicted. You must stand the test.

*[For it is He] Who rescued and saved us from such a perilous death, and He will still rescue and save us; in and on Him we have set our hope (our joyful and confident expectation) that He will again deliver us [from danger and destruction and draw us to Himself].*
                                    *—2 Corinthians 1:10* AMP

Even while I was sick and dealing with the mental effects of being sick, I was still receiving requests for prayer for cousins and friends who did not know I was stuck in bed most days. What did I do? I honored their requests. I found this to be a good time to admit some faults and pray for them while I was in the infirmary.

*Confess your faults one to another, and pray one for another, that ye may be healed.*                              *—James 5:16a*

As I stated earlier, the devil often attacks you in your body when he cannot break your spirit, causing you to become ill. You have to know that your times and seasons are in the hands of the Lord and they shall not be altered or adjusted by anyone or anything. God will come through with healing while giving you the correct understanding and interpretation of the divine movement going on in your life. The plan will be revealed to you. You have been bought with a price and no sickness or disease will overtake you.

*And the prayer of faith shall save the sick, and the Lord shall raise him up; and if he have committed sins, they shall be forgiven him.*
*—James 5:15*

Jesus healed many that were blind, and not with the same method. We don't all get healed the same way. Healing is progressive at times, because one touch doesn't always do it. No matter what sickness you have, present it to God. Do not hide it, be like the man who stretched forth his withered hand and received restoration. There is a standard of complete restoration. In Mark 3:3, Jesus is telling us to stand forth in our faith then He tells us to stretch forth to receive healing.

### Overflow Scripture Meditations

*Blessed is he that considereth the poor: the LORD will deliver him in time of trouble. The LORD will preserve him, and keep him alive; and he shall be blessed upon the earth: and thou wilt not deliver him unto the will of his enemies.* *—Psalm 41:1-3*

*Here my voice, O God, in my complaint; guard and preserve my life from the terror of the enemy.* *—Psalm 64:1 AMP*

*Blotting out the handwriting of ordinances that was against us, which was contrary to us, and took it out of the way, nailing it to his cross.*
                                                    —*Colossians 2:14*

**ADVERSITY IS THE GREAT UNIVERSITY. ADVERSITY ADDED A VERSE TO ME.**

*Jentzen Franklin*

# Prayer changes everything

*And he spake a parable unto them to this end, that men ought always to pray, and not to faint.*
*—Luke 18:1*

Jesus told his disciples a story to illustrate their need for constant prayer and to show them that they must keep praying until the answer comes. Prayer is a two-way conversation. Tell God everything that is on your heart. Listen carefully, and use your Bible as you pray because as you meditate in prayer, God will speak to you through the pages. God's Word is the bread of life, and you lifting the bread up to God and blessing it is your prayer.

Prayer keeps you connected to God and places you in a position to ask Him about what's going on in your life at any given time. This exchange between you and God will change your perspective and you will see things the way He does. God's ways and thoughts are higher than ours. Therefore when you pray and began to see things more clearly, everything changes. Your thoughts change, your attitude changes, your joy changes, your praise changes. Are you getting this? Prayer changes everything! During prayer we can ask God about the work He is already doing in our lives, and ask for specific things we want His hand on in our lives. Isaiah 45:11 states, "Ask me of things to come concerning my sons, and concerning the works of my hands; command ye me."

If you need wisdom, understanding, and answers in the midst of your trial, asks God in prayer and He will supply what you need. Believers do not have to grope around in the dark, hoping to stumble upon answers. We can ask God to grant us the ability to make wise decisions in difficult circumstances. The Bible tells us that wisdom is the principle thing and that we should get it from God. The Proverbs were written by King Solomon of Israel, David's son, and he wrote them to teach his people how to live and how to act in every circumstance. Instead of acting or reacting in a ungodly manner, because of leaning on your own understanding, you take your concerns to God in prayer first and He will guide your every step toward peace and safety, giving you wisdom. This equates to knowledge and understanding. Wisdom will show you how to distinguish right from wrong, and how to make the right decision every time.

*If any of you lack wisdom, let him ask of God, that giveth to all men liberally . . . and it shall be given him.*      **—James 1:5**

Things will change for the better; when you pray things have to change. Your thoughts will change, and your understanding will change. Prayer also puts the angelic host to work (see Genesis 18:1 and 19-29), allowing them to war on our behalf, protecting us from the unseen, and ministering to us in our hour of need.

We fight against spirits and not people. This sometimes can be difficult to remember because the spirit works through people, making the people appear to be the enemy. However, when you stand in prayer, you will be reminded of where the fight really belongs, in the spirit. God waits right by the door of your spirit to speak with you and to eat with you. Prayer is where you get the answers you need.

When you pray the Scriptures, you will hear the voice behind the Word. In Acts 22:7, Saul heard the voice. John 10:4 tells us that His sheep know His voice, because they have become accustomed to following Him. God walks ahead of us, showing us the way if we will only follow. If you listen, you will hear His voice and open up to Him, and He will lead you and you will follow Him. Just the posture of praying indicates you are following God. You must follow God to hear His voice. Listen, if you open the door to let God in, He will share a meal with you just as a friend would do.

*Behold, I stand at the door, and knock: if any man hear my voice, and open the door, I will come in to him, and will sup with him, and he with me.*     —*Revelation 3:20*

When you pray, reinforcements and assistance will be made available to you. God will contend with those who contend with you. He will close up the way of those who pursue and persecute you. You will be able to run through troops and leap over walls. When you feel vulnerable, you can pray for strength and protection. He will hide you in the cleft of the rock. God will make your way perfect. He will give you stability so that you are able to stand firmly and make progress while walking the dangerous heights, as Jesus was, of testing and trouble.

*Pray without ceasing. In every thing give thanks: for this is the will of God in Christ Jesus concerning you.*     —*1 Thessalonians 5:17-18*

Remember, you do not fight spiritual battles in your own strength; you fight them in the strength of the Lord. God will set you securely upon your high place in Him, causing you to see from a higher perspective and hear the instructions for the battle you are facing. He will teach your hands to war and your fingers to fight. He is your rock, your shield, and your strong tower. When the enemy comes in like a flood, God will lift up a standard against him. You may not feel like anything is happening, but do you remember when Daniel was praying for 21 days? Something was happening during the time he could not see. Daniel could not feel the changes that were occurring. The angelic host was fighting the demonic forces that did not want to see Daniel get the victory.

Occasionally you will find yourself up against a brick wall. Big and intimidating, tall and slick, you can't push through it, climb over it, or see your way around it. That is when prayer gets innovative. You pray for ways to get beyond that wall. Luke 11:5-13 teaches us about being persistent in prayer. We advance in life through prayer. Peace and contentment are yours when you pray. You gain comprehension, which is a working knowledge, when you pray. Sometimes the answer to prayer comes in the form of a process. Most of us do not want to go through the process of getting our prayers answered. God is going to tell you to do something that will lead you into the end result of your prayer. God wants to develop something in you so that you will be able to enjoy the prize. The answer sends you on a course to what you have prayed for.

*Prove all things; hold fast that which is good. —1 Thessalonians 5:21*

Prayer is the place where you can destroy the works of the devil. You can shut the devil up with all his lies. When you use the Word of God in prayer, you are resisting the devil and every evil thing he is coming against you with… Search Scriptures to counterattack the attack, use them in your prayers. You must fight every thought and everything that does not line up with the Word of God. Fight with the Word of God, this is your sword. You wield this sword with your hands, and God has said that He will teach your hands to war. This tells me that your words must be God's words. Again God's Word is a double-edged sword, able to be used by you in prayer and in your speech. Prayer reminds you that you are more than a conqueror.

"Why doesn't God answer my prayers?" We often ask this question, especially in the crucial moments of our lives. The answer to this question can be found in the intimacy one develops by communicating with God. Jesus prayed to God and received answers.

The disciples asked Jesus, "Lord, teach us to pray" (Luke 11:1). The disciples knew about praying and had probably prayed many times.

But they noticed something different about the way Jesus prayed. His prayers had a power that intrigued them. He prayed as though He expected an answer—because He did! You keep speaking the Word, and you keep it up until full faith comes then you pray. The disciples' request indicates that there is a right way and a wrong way to pray, and it is important for us to know the difference. John 14:13-14 lets us know that if we ask anything in Jesus' name, He will do it. To pray in Jesus' name does not mean that you tack His Holy Name onto your wish list. It means that your prayers are consistent with what Jesus Himself would pray about in a particular situation. 1 John 5:14 lets us know that we should pray according to the Word and the will of God. The Word and the will of God are synonymous. To pray for anything not promised in the Word of God is a waste of time, but to pray for what we know is God's desire is a absolute winner!

*Faithful is he that calleth you, who also will do it.*
*—1 Thessalonians 5:24*

When you face battles, get on your knees and pray. Do not get discouraged, pray until you get the answers. This is called "praying through." Pray aloud, using simple, natural words. You do not have to impress God with your vocabulary or your spirituality. Talk to God in your own language; He understands it. For most of your prayer, give thanks to God for the answers that you know, in faith, are coming. 1 Peter 5:7 tells us to cast all of our cares upon Him, for He cares for us. Pray for people you dislike or who have mistreated you to ensure no resentment sets in. Find another believer and ask that person to join you in prayer for God's answer. The Bible says that if two of you agree on earth concerning anything that they shall ask, it will be done for them by My father in heaven.

*Again I say unto you, That if two of you shall agree on earth as touching any thing that they shall ask, it shall be done for them of my Father which is in heaven. For where two or three are gathered together in my name, there am I in the midst of them.*     **—Matthew 18:19-20**

There is another aspect of praying that utilizes your most holy faith, and that is praying in tongues. Praying in a language that you do not understand places you in a mystery. The mysteries of God can be made known to you by praying this way. This will help tremendously when you do not know what to pray. When your heart is feeling really low and you do not know what to do, praying in the Spirit is the answer. When you are a chosen believer, situations are going to occur that may be simply mind blowing. You may find yourself in a circumstance or situation that literally drops you to your knees in tears, and you have no one to turn to. Every now and then you may experience the type of pain that will not cease or subside even though you sing, smile, and dance. The pain just keeps coming back and reminding you that you are vulnerable and human. You have tried to hide from it and have tried to tell it to go. Remember, praying with your own understanding may not be deep enough to give you relief. When this happens; you are being prompted to allow the Holy Spirit to search the deep things of God. Praying in tongues will allow the Holy Spirit to intercede on your behalf. The Holy Spirit knows the mind of Christ and the will of God.

The Holy Spirit causes us to speak the will of God. (See 2 Samuel 23:3.) Speaking the will of God is speaking the Words of God—proclaiming what you want to see—proclaiming "let there be." Proclamation which is dependent on the Spirit is seen to be independent of human understanding. (See Mark 13:11.) For it is not you who speaks, but the Holy Spirit. When you allow the Spirit to speak, you will begin to know the ways of God more perfectly. When you are driven to the point of despair, remember that the greater the opposition, the greater the power that is available to you.

*For if I pray in an unknown tongue, my spirit prayeth, my understanding is unfruitful.*     **—1 Corinthians 14:14**

Praying in the Spirit places you in a position to receive God's wisdom. Paul tells us that great wisdom is for mature Christians, chosen believers who have been made mature by the fiery trials they've faced. The glories of heaven are available to you, and you get let in on God's wise plan. This wisdom empowers you to become solid, immovable, assured, knowing, firm, and gives you the ability to stand.

*Howbeit we speak wisdom among them that are perfect: yet not the wisdom of this world, nor of the princes of this world, that come to nought: but we speak the wisdom of God in a mystery, even the hidden wisdom, which God ordained before the world unto our glory.*     **—1 Corinthians 2:6-7**

Speaking and praying in tongues means that you are tapping into the mysteries of God. The Holy Spirit utters secret truths and hidden things that must be caught in the spirit. This qualifies you as a wise person. I have a few words about wise people I would like to share.

*The mouth of a righteous man is a well of life.*     **—Proverbs 10:11**

This is living truth. Wisdom builds her house and hewn out her seven pillars, causing the devil to flee seven different ways.

*The words of a man's mouth are as deep waters, And the wellspring of wisdom as a flowing brook.*     **—Proverbs 18:4**

Deep waters are plenteous, heavy, and difficult to fathom. The wellspring is a fountain of sparkling fresh, pure, life-giving, gushing streams.

*Counsel in the heart of man is like deep water; But a man of understanding will draw it out.* —***Proverbs 20:5***

*So too the [Holy] Spirit comes to our aid and bears us up in our weakness; for we do not know what prayer to offer nor how to offer it worthily as we ought, but the Spirit Himself goes to meet our supplication and pleads in our behalf with unspeakable yearnings and groanings too deep for utterance.* —***Romans 8:26***

What better prayer partner to have than the Holy Spirit Himself? Some trials and problems leave you so troubled and confused, they seem to be getting worse, not better, and so, not knowing how to pray, you groan. Groaning can be likened to a mother in the labor room. The mother is in agony because the pain is so intense, but she knows this agony has a purpose. With every contraction and every groan, the baby within is saying "Birth me out of here!" Likewise, as the Spirit groans on your behalf, the closer your getting to a new birth from God.

*Yet to us God has unveiled and revealed them by and through His Spirit, for the [Holy] Spirit searches diligently, exploring and examining everything, even sounding the profound and bottomless things of God [the divine counsels and things hidden and beyond man's scrutiny].* —***1 Corinthians 2:10*** AMP

God invites us to pray about critical matters like forgiveness, the increasing of our faith, deliverance, and healing. God also asks us to cast our cares on Him.

Prayerlessness is sin. At pivotal moments in your life, prayer should be your first choice, not your last gasp. Remember, as powerful as God is, He does not answer prayer until you pray.

*Far be it from me that I should sin against the Lord in ceasing to pray for you.*               *—1 Samuel 12.23* AMP

David, who consistently dealt with wars, always went to God in prayer for new instructions and strategies. When you are in the midst of a battle, there God will be training you for victory. Prayer will let you know what to bind and rebuke. You will bring to a halt and prohibit the unwanted aggravation satan causes while in battle when you pray. False burdens will be lifted and feelings of heaviness will be removed. Prayer can go anywhere and everywhere. Prayer can go into the boss' office, into the court room, into the boardroom, and into the intensive care unit—anytime and all the time—day or night; even while you sleep. There are no limits on prayer.

Everything that stands in the way of your victory over affliction will be broken off your life by prayer and obedience. Your obedience to stand in faith is vital to all victories. Your obedience to God's instructions from prayer is vital to victory. Anything that is contrary to or hinders the fulfillment of God's purpose for your life will be shattered as you obey your instructions in prayer. The sword of the Lord will sever any and all curses and deceptions. Prayer will help you to resist the wiles of the devil. You will prevail against all limitations.

*The earnest prayer of a righteous person has great power and wonderful results.*                  *—James 5:16a* NLT

*Wherefore take unto you the whole armor of God that ye may be able to withstand in the evil day, and having done all to stand. Stand therefore, having your loins gird about with truth [to protect your integrity]; and having n the breastplate of righteousness; [to protect your reputation]; and your feet shod with the preparation of the gospel of peace [to guide your every step]; above all, taking the shield of faith [which secures your future and destiny]; wherewith ye shall be able to quench all the fiery darts of the wicked. And take he helmet of salvation [to protect your mind] and the sword of the Spirit, which is the word of God [which grants you dominion and authority]: Praying always with all manner of prayer and supplication in the Spirit, and watching thereunto with all perseverance and supplication for all saints.*

**—Ephesians 6:13-18 [inserts added]**

Effective prayer is prayer that attains what it seeks. It is prayer that moves God, effecting its end.          ***Charles G. Finney***

## Overflow Scripture Meditations

*After this manner therefore pray ye: Our father which art in heaven, Hallowed be name. Thy kingdom come. Thy will be done in earth, as it is in heaven. Give us this day our daily bread. And forgive us our debts, as we forgive our debtors. And lead us not into temptation, but deliver us from evil: for thine is the kingdom, and the power, and the glory, for ever. Amen.*          **—Matthew 6:9-13**

*For he that speaketh in an unknown tongue speaketh not unto men, but unto God: for no man understandeth him; howbeit in the spirit he speaketh mysteries.*          **—1 Corinthians 14:2**

*Ask of me, and I shall give thee the heathen for thine inheritance, and the uttermost parts of the earth for thy possession.*          **—Psalm 2:8**

I BELIEVE THAT YOU CAN NEVER
TAKE A BREAK FROM GREATNESS
—AND RELATIONSHIPS OFFER
THE HIGHEST OPPORTUNITY
FOR ACHIEVING GREATNESS.

*Tyrese Gibson*

# I CHOSE YOU

*For many are called, but few are chosen.*              —*Matthew 22:14*

God calls many Christians to join Him in His work on the earth. A few of the called Christians get chosen to do the work. You may ask, "Chosen to do what?" To accomplish, to act, to deliver, to repair the breach, to save your family, to break the curse, to reach a nation—these are things you may have been chosen for. You may have been chosen to be a trailblazer for your children. Many Christians are called to do the will of the Lord, but only a few show up ready to be chosen.

We, the church, are the bride of Christ. As a bride, you are supposed to wear bridal clothing. When God invites or summons you to a particular assignment, you must have on the proper garments. God calls many to work with him as contributors to the world of faith, but few show up with the proper clothing. The Bible tells us to clothe ourselves with the armor of God, to put on the garment of praise, and to robe ourselves with righteousness. This is how you become chosen. Noah was chosen to build the ark; David was chosen to slay Goliath and to be king. When God raises you up, no one can pull you down. No devil in hell can prevail against God's decision to choose you.

*Behold, I have refined you, but not as silver; I have tried and chosen you in the furnace of affliction. For My own sake, for My own sake, I do it [I refrain and do not utterly destroy you]; for why should I permit My name to be polluted and profaned [which it would be if the Lord completely destroyed His chosen people]? And I will not give My glory to another [by permitting the worshipers of idols to triumph over you].*
                                        —*Isaiah 48:10-11* AMP

When you have been chosen to perform at a higher standard, purging is necessary. Purging is a harsh cleansing and is necessary to rid you of any impurities that cannot go with you to the next assignment. God does this for His sake and for His purpose. The act of purification must occur for the benefit of you and others that God has placed in your realm of influence. To be refined means to make or become pure. Refining is the process to get rid of unsuitable elements—to make or become more elegant or polished. A furnace is an appliance for producing heat. When things began to get hot for you in your life, the devil has turned up the heat in the fiery furnace hoping to burn you up, but God is with you in the fire. Therefore you will not even smell like smoke when you come out. (See Daniel 3:22-27.) When the devil is coming at you with everything he's got, you are in the fiery furnace. This is the place where God will choose to refine you. Oh yes, the devil means it for bad, but God will take this opportunity to make it good, causing you to be exalted afterwards. God chooses us in the "furnace of affliction," because He knows we'll come out stronger than we were before the refining process.

The purging experience is necessary if we are going to move into a higher place in God. Before Jesus gave up His spirit, He came to a point in Matthew 27:46 when His strength was almost gone. This is a picture of the purging process. You feel as though God has left you to fend for yourself. The devil would like for you to believe that God has forgotten about you or does not care what happens to you.

*My God, My God, why have You abandoned Me [leaving Me helpless, forsaking and failing Me in my need]?*
*—Matthew 27:46* AMP

Interestingly enough, the Bible tells us to be joyful in our troubles. How do we do that? Be ever mindful of the end of a thing. Know that you win in the end. Rejoice in the Lord; sing and speak praises to

Him; lift up holy hands and dance like David. This will give you the strength you need to get through. Think about how good God will make the end of your endurance, and thank Him for it. This is how your faith is proved.

*Consider it wholly joyful, my brethren, whenever you are enveloped in or encounter trials of any sort or fall into various temptations. Be assured and understand that the trial and proving of your faith bring out endurance and steadfastness and patience. But let endurance and steadfastness and patience have full play and do a thorough work, so that you may be . . . perfectly and fully developed [ with no defects], lacking in nothing.*

*—James 1:2-4* AMP

Letting this process play out to the full is of vital importance. If you let the caterpillar out during the struggling stage of transformation, it will die and never get to fly as a butterfly. During the time of intense struggle, the caterpillar is going through a metamorphosis. In other words, a transformation is taking place. Once this stage is complete, a perfect and fully developed, lacking nothing, butterfly emerges and begins to fly beautifully and gloriously.

*From Mount Zion, the perfection of beauty, God shines in glorious radiance.*      *—Psalm 50:2* NLT

When an attack comes your way, know that there is protection for those that have been chosen to accomplish the will of God. Many times we get hit off guard or in a blind spot. It is hard to understand that the devil wants to steal the double portion that has been set aside just for you, chosen one, but it is true. The devil knows that if you endure affliction, "double for your trouble" shall be given to you.

*Instead of shame and dishonor, you shall have a double portion of
prosperity and everlasting joy.*      —*Isaiah 61:7* TLB

The best way out is always through. Through the flood, and
through the fire, the Lord promises to be with you. He promises to
get you to the other side of whatever you are in. When you have been
chosen for a battle, the outcome is victory every time.

*When you pass through the waters, I will be with you, and through the
rivers, they will not overwhelm you. When you walk through fire, you
will not be burned or scorched, nor will the flame kindle upon you.*
     —*Isaiah 43:2* AMP

Whenever God gets ready to elevate you, He must first introduce
you to an enemy. The more important your future, the greater your
opponent will be. Never let the size of your enemy, the massiveness of
his strength, or the volume of his threats intimidate you. The size of
your enemy is a measure of the size of God's confidence in your ability to overcome. The larger and more powerful the enemy, the more
potential there is for elevation in your life. You can never become
who you are supposed to be without victory, and there is no victory
without a battle. The bigger the battle, the greater the victory! Esther
had Haaman, Moses had Pharaoh, and Hannah had Peninnah.

*Indeed all who delight in piety and are determined to live a devoted and
godly life in Christ Jesus will meet with persecution.*
     —*2 Timothy 3:12* AMP

When your enemy is in your area of influence, his only purpose
is to steal, kill, and destroy. He is a thief who wants to steal your
strength, kill your present, and destroy our future.

Let us examine and learn from the principles found in the book
of Esther. Esther being a bride and a queen and learned to appease

king Axzereus by focusing on what he desired. This gave her favor with him. (Listen to this, because this is a principle to heed in your relationship with God.) As you keep your focus on God, He prepares a table before you in the presence of your enemies. Esther invited Haaman (her enemy) to a meal she prepared for her king. Learn to worship God while the enemy is at your table. It has already been prepared. Invite your enemy because the right hand knows not what the left hand is doing. Esther did exactly this and obtained victory over Haaman.

The same night or season of affliction that satan plans your demise, your King is planning your reward! The King Who never sleeps nor slumbers has gone ahead of you to make the crooked places in your life straight and the rough places in your life smooth. God makes sure that everything works together for your good. God is looking for a chance to humiliate the enemy of your destiny. Before it's all over, satan will be confessing that Jesus Christ is Lord!

*Wherefore the rather, brethren, give diligence to make your calling and election sure: for if ye do these things, ye shall never fall.*
*—2 Peter 1:10*

He chose to call you, and because He called you, you are committed. He called you into the commitment. Do not give up. You were chosen to survive, to succeed, and to be significant.

*Ye have not chosen me, but I have chosen you, and ordained you, that ye should go and bring forth fruit, and that your fruit should remain: that whatsoever ye shall ask of the father in my name, he may give it you.*
*—John 15:16*

## Overflow Scripture Meditations

*Who shall bring any charge against God's elect [when it is] God Who justifies [that is, Who puts us in right relation to Himself? Who shall come forward and accuse or impeach those whom God has chosen? Will God, Who acquits us?] Who is there to condemn [us]? Will Christ Jesus (the Messiah), Who died, or rather Who was raised from the dead, Who is at the right hand of God actually pleading as He intercedes for us? Who shall ever separate us from Christ's love? Shall suffering and affliction and tribulation? Or calamity and distress? Or persecution or hunger or destitution or peril or sword? Even as it is written, For Thy sake we are put to death all the day long; we are regarded and counted as sheep for the slaughter. Yet amid all these things we are more than conquerors and gain a surpassing victory through Him Who loved us.*

*—Romans 8:33-37* AMP

*According as His divine power hath given unto us all things that pertain unto life and godliness, through the knowledge of Him that hath called us to glory and virtue.* *—2 Peter 1:3*

DIAMONDS DO NOT SPARKLE UNLESS THEY ARE CUT. ROSES DO NOT RELEASE THEIR FRAGRANCE UNLESS THEY ARE CRUSHED. A SEED DOES NOT TAKE ROOT UNLESS IT FALLS TO THE GROUND, AND STARS DO NOT SHINE UNTIL THE DARKEST HOUR.

*Dr. Millicent Hunter*

# FORMED AND APPROVED

*"Before I formed you in the womb I knew you, before you were born I set you apart."* —*Jeremiah 1:5* NIV

You have God's approval, which means you have official permission to exercise your faith according to His calling. You have been sanctioned and sanctified, which means you are "set apart for a special purpose." Being set apart for a special purpose includes your right to exercise your inherent power. The power that God has given you is for a special purpose.

God says He already knew you before you were born. To know someone means to have intimate knowledge of their proclivities and personality traits. God knows exactly who you are, with all your shortcomings, and has set you apart to work with Him. What applied to the prophet Jeremiah in this regard applies to you as well. We too are working it out.

*For those whom He foreknew [of whom He was aware and loved beforehand], He also destined from the beginning [foreordaining them] to be molded into the image of His Son [and share inwardly His likeness], that He might become the firstborn among many brethren. And those whom He thus foreordained, He also called; and those whom He called, He also justified. And those whom He justified, he also glorified [raising them to a heavenly dignity and condition or state of being].*
—*Romans 8:29-30* AMP

God approved of you before anybody else ever got a chance to disapprove you. That is great news. Going through whatever you face, standing tall in your spirit while suffering unjustly, grants you favor from God. Passing the tests grants you approval from God. Receiving approval from God means you do not need anyone else's approval and the victorious crown is yours. Imagine walking around with a beautiful crown of victory on your head, signifying you are worthy.

*Blessed (happy, to be envied) is the man who is patient under trial and stands up under temptation, for when he has stood the test and been approved, he will receive [the victor's] crown of life which God has promised to those who love Him.* —*James 1:12* AMP

Wearing this crown of life is reason enough to consistently give praise to God. Thanking God for everything, at all times, under every circumstance, ushers us into praising His name. Praising His name ushers us into worship. Make up in your mind that you will sincerely thank the Lord at all times.

*Through Him, therefore, let us constantly and at all times offer up to God a sacrifice of praise, which is the fruit of lips that thankfully acknowledge and confess and glorify His name.* —*Hebrews 13:15* AMP

Formed in the likeness of God and being made in His image, gives us our true identity. Remember this whenever the devil tries to tell you otherwise. You are fearfully and wonderfully made. The devil will try to give you an identity crisis like he tried with Jesus in the wilderness. You must know who you are and whose you are. Your world is determined by your thoughts; what you think about yourself is crucial.

*For You did form my inward parts; You did knit me together in my mother's womb. I will confess and praise You for You are fearful and wonderful and for the awful wonder of my birth! Wonderful are You works, and that my inner self knows right well.* —*Psalm 139:13-14* AMP

In the secret place, the hidden place, the mysterious place, in the deep earthly place, the cells that make up your body were put together to form you in the likeness and image of God.

*My frame was not hidden from You when I was being formed in secret [and] intricately and curiously wrought [as if embroidered with various colors] in the depths of the earth [a region of darkness and mystery].*
         *—Psalm 139:15* AMP

God was watching the atoms come together to make the person you were to be and recorded the length of days you would be given.

*Your eyes saw my unformed substance, and in Your book all the days [of my life] were written before ever they took shape, when as yet there was none of them.*         *—Psalm 139:16* AMP

God has you on His mind, He thinks about you in an awesome precious way, all the time. You cannot number the many thoughts He has for and about you. He is God Almighty!

*How precious and weighty also are Your thoughts to me, O God! How vast is the sum of them. If I could count them, they would be more in number than the sand.*         *—Psalm 139:17-18* AMP

You cannot move beyond trouble until you understand who you are. There is a place so far within you that the Word calls it "the deep." When you are in trouble, cry out to God from that deep place within. God placed this deepness within us all.

*[Roaring] deep [roaring] calls to deep at the thunder of Your waterspouts; all Your breakers and Your rolling waves have gone over me.*         *—Psalm 42:7* AMP

God formed you, approved you, and set you apart for a special purpose. He thinks about you all the time, will never leave you, and will protect you as He teaches you to stand in faith by His love toward you as you go through fire and flood. Amen!

*Listen to me, O isles and coastlands, and hearken, you peoples from afar. The Lord has called me from the womb; from the body of my mother He has named my name. And He has made my mouth like a sharp sword; in the shadow of His hand has He hid me and made me a polished arrow; in his quiver has He kept me close and concealed me.*

*—Isaiah 49:1-2* AMP

God loves you and I; He has loved us from the beginning.

*A glorious throne, set on high from the beginning, is the place of our sanctuary ( the temple).*     *—Jeremiah 17:12* AMP

### Overflow Scripture Meditations

*Offer to God the sacrifice of thanksgiving, and pay your vow to the Most High, and call on Me in the day of trouble; I will deliver you, and you shall honor and glorify Me.*     *—Psalm 50:14-15* AMP

*In Him we also were made [God's] heritage (portion) and we obtained an inheritance; for we had been foreordained (chosen and appointed beforehand) in accordance with His purpose, Who works out everything in agreement with the counsel and design of His [own] will.*

*—Ephesians 1:11* AMP

*Yet, O Lord, You are our Father; we are the clay, and You the Potter, and we are all the work of Your hand.*     *—Isaiah 64:8* AMP

*Poverty and shame shall be to him that refuseth instruction: but he that regardeth reproof shall be honored.*       **—Proverbs 13:18**

*Apply thine heart unto instruction, and thine ears to the words of knowledge.*       **—Proverbs 23:12**

# THE HOLY SPIRIT IS THE MOST IMPORTANT PERSON ON EARTH.

*Dr. Myles Monroe*

# HE'LL PROTECT YOU

*The Lord protects them and keeps them alive. He gives them prosperity in the land and rescues them from their enemies.        —Psalm 41:2 NLT*

Your promise of protection is all through the Bible. In this chapter we will focus on the protection found in Psalm 91. Here we find God breaking it down from on high showing you how to receive this awesome promise. You must remain stable and fixed under the shadow of the One whose power no foe can withstand. Trusting in God means you lean on Him, rely on Him, and have your confidence in Him. When trouble comes knocking at your door, answer by saying what the Lord is to you—your Protector. Speak about how God is your hiding place and your safety place. When you trust God with your heart and say it with your mouth. He is sure to protect your spirit during a trial and your mind from the pestilence buzzing around in your head. Not only are you protected by God, this promise also comes with deliverance.

*He that dwelleth in the secret place of the most High shall abide under the shadow of the Almighty. I will say of the LORD, He is my refuge and my fortress: my God, in him will I trust. Surely he shall deliver thee from the snare of the fowler, and from the noisome pestilence.*
                                        *—Psalm 91:1-3*

The truth of God's protection will defend you against any and all attacks coming from the enemy of your soul, spirit, and body. He promises to cover you with protection as you trust Him and stand with Him in faith and love. God's Word is truth,  I encourage you to keep this promise of protection close to you when things get really tough. Remember, instead of worrying about your circumstances or situation, God will give you sweet sleep.

*He shall cover thee with his feathers, and under his wings shalt thou
trust: his truth shall be thy shield and buckler.*     **—Psalm 91:4**

During the day, things are coming at you from many angles:
bad news, negative reports, evil wishes, slanders, and the like. These
things are like arrows, aimed with a sharp point to hurt you. Dealing with character assassinators that walk and stalk in darkness to
destroy your name and reputation causes you to need God's protection at all times. By the time night falls and you are ready to retire
for the evening, fear can strike your heart as your mind goes through
your day trying to make sense of all that happened to and around
you. God is telling you not to be afraid of this. He knows what you
have been through and wants you to know that He is covering you,
protecting you, and defending you.

*Thou shall not be afraid for the terror by night; nor the arrows that
flieth by day; nor for the pestilence that walketh in darkness; nor for the
destruction that wasteth at noonday.*     **—Psalm 91:5-6**

Remember that it is vitally important to stay very close to God.
That is what the Scriptures mean when it tells you to dwell in the
secret place of the Most High. You yourself will be inaccessible in the
secret place of God. God will cover you up like a mother eagle covers her babies. The mother eagle covers her babies by spreading her
feathers over them. The devil may seem to have an advantage, but
that is only because he has the power to deceive, accuse, and tempt.
However, greater is the power invested in you by God. Therefore, be
not afraid.

*A thousand shall fall at thy side, and ten thousand at thy right hand, but
it shall not come nigh thee. Only with thine eyes shalt thou behold and
see the reward of the wicked. Because thou hast made the LORD, which is
thy refuge, even the most High, thy habitation; there shall no evil befall*

*thee, neither shall any plague come nigh thy dwelling.*
*—Psalm 91:7-10*

The Word also tells us of the angels that guard and fight on our behalf. The angels guard and fight for our answers to prayer to get through to us. In Genesis, we see God using angels to guard the Tree of Life. No one can get access to that Tree illegally. We see in Daniel how God used angels to fight for Daniel's prayer to be answered, (See Daniel 10:12-14.) We cannot see these angels, but we are surrounded with them as they wait to hearken to the voice of God to do His will.

In another story from in Daniel, we see three of God's people in big trouble with the government. They were faithful to God. They abided in Him. When they were faced with danger, instead of worrying about it, they spoke words of faith. "Our God is able to deliver us!" (See Daniel 3:17.) As these men were thrown into the burning, fiery furnace, a fourth man was walking in the midst of the fire with them in the form of the Son of God. The Bible tells us that afterwards, not even a "hair of their head was singed, neither were their coats changed, nor the smell of fire had passed on them" (Daniel 3:27). That is protection! Hebrews 1:14 AMP says "are not the angels all ministering spirits (servants) sent out in the service [of God for the assistance] of those who are to inherit salvation?" When angels appear to people, "Fear not" is usually the first words out of their mouths.

*For he shall give his angels charge over thee, To keep thee in all thy ways. They shall bear thee up in their hands, Lest thou dash thy foot against a stone.*    *—Psalm 91:11-12*

Loving the Lord has protection power you need to receive deliverance. Setting your love on our Father in heaven causes Him to deliver you out of every bit of trouble you find yourself in willingly and unwillingly. Knowing God as Protector allows Him to set you up in a very high place far above your predicament. Knowing with understanding that God is protecting you at all times, especially in bad times, places you on top of, not under, your circumstances. God has several names that describe who He is, and knowing God as Protector has great benefits.

*Thou shalt tread upon the lion and adder: the young lion and the dragon shalt thou trample under feet. Because he hath set his love upon me, therefore will I deliver him: I will set him on high, because he hath known my name.* —***Psalm 91:13-14***

Developing a personal relationship with God while going through the fire and the flood causes you to know and understand God's love more. Your understanding of the Love of God qualifies you for deliverance from whatever you are facing. Again we can look at Daniel, who had to come face to face with a den of lions. Daniel was a member of the royal staff of Persia second only to the king himself. Daniel had so much influence that other presidents and princes became jealous of his position and began to look for ways to remove him from authority. And no matter how hard they looked, "they could find none occasion nor fault; forasmuch as he was faithful (Daniel 6:4). Daniel was chosen and was also faithful both to God and to King Darius. When a law was passed that forbade him to pray to God, he remained faithful, knowing he risked being thrown into the den of lions. Since Daniel continually served God out of love, he qualified for the protection of God. Daniel was to be tried. Prior to going into the den, the king said to Daniel, "May your God, whom you are serving continually, deliver you!" Deliverance came by way of an angel. Because Daniel believed in, relied on, and trusted God, no hurt came to him. Afterwards the king destroyed Daniel's enemies and honored Daniel's God.

*He shall call upon me, and I will answer him: I will be with him in*
*trouble; I will deliver him, and honor him.*     —*Psalm 91:15*

God sent His angel to shut the mouths of the lions in that den with
Daniel. God delivered Daniel because he always delivers and protects those who love Him. King Darius had already set his thoughts
on promoting Daniel over the whole realm of his kingdom. However,
the other presidents, princes, counselors, and captains were plotting
to take Daniel down. King Darius was manipulated into signing a
decree that would test Daniel and himself. They both passed the test,
and Daniel received honor from God and the king. (See Daniel 6:25-
28.) You can trust God with your life; He'll do the same thing for you
He did for Daniel. When you know God and love God, you can call
on God for deliverance and honor.

Protection is a great benefit that comes with deliverance and long
life. There is a big difference between knowing something to be true
in your head and experiencing the reality in your life. You could have
the concept in your mind because you heard it or read it, however,
experiencing it personally gives you understanding.

With every beautiful rose, there are thorns. The thorns protect
the rose. Beautiful things are always accompanied by challenges. Everything that is precious to God is protected by God. Being tried
and chosen, formed and approved, qualifies you to be protected and
delivered from every fire and every flood.

When God wanted to deliver Noah from the destruction about
to come, He instructed him to build an ark. That ark was to protect
him and keep him safe while the whole world was perishing around
him.

I believe God is telling us the same thing today, "Build an ark
made out of the Word of God." What you know from the Word of

God will protect and save you while all hell is breaking loose. These are the Words you will be standing on during your times of adversity, and you have to know what to stand on. You have to believe the promise of protection. You cannot have faith for something you do not know and understand.

*With long life will I satisfy him, and show him my salvation.*
*—Psalm 91:16*

## Overflow Scripture Meditations

*The Lord will keep you from all evil; He will keep your life.*
*—Psalm 121:7* AMP

CONSIDER YOUR TIMES OF STRUGGLE,
TESTING, AND TEMPTATION AS
DIVINE OPPORTUNITIES TO BE
TRAINED IN THE ART OF STRATEGIC
PRAYER AND SPIRITUAL WARFARE.

*Cindy Trimm*

# THE TEST

*Beloved, do not be amazed and bewildered at the fiery ordeal which is taking place to test your quality, as though something strange (unusual and alien to you and your position) were befalling you.*

*1 Peter 4:12* AMP

The education system, beginning in grade school and at every level, requires us to take tests to reveal how much we were able to retain during our course of learning. These tests also show our preparation for the next assignment; they are the gatekeepers of appointment to a higher level. In our Christian walk, beginning at conversion and at every level of spiritual growth afterwards, we are required to take spiritual tests to recognize and increase our level of faith.

Spiritual tests indicate how well we are prepared to go on, to move up in God, and to take on greater responsibility. When you want to be blessed by God and used of God, you must go through something to prove your durability. When Jesus said, "Oh ye of little faith," He was referring to your lasting faith during a test. God allows testing in our lives. These tests are not to determine our level of faith; God knows our level of faith. No, the test allows us to see ourselves as God sees us—our real level of commitment and our spiritual maturity.

God cannot use wimpy people who run away at the first sign of trouble and run scared at the tiniest of challenges. Anybody can shout with joy when there is money in the bank, peace in the home, gas in the car, and food on the table. Testimonies come easy when there is joy in our hearts and love in our lives. Yet when struggles come and our heart is breaking, God wants to know if we can still sing, teach, preach, and serve. Can we do what God has called us to do when there is trouble all around us? Then, and only then, our true level of commitment and faith is revealed.

Are you willing to sacrifice who you are now, in order to become who God has called you to be? If you say no, you will remain stagnant in your current level, never experiencing the result of change or the beauty of growth. For a chosen believer, change is a necessary and perpetual facet of life.

The longest test I had to endure lasted for a year and four months. Prior to that, I was feeling great, I mean, just wonderful about my life. I saw the promises of God being manifested in my business and my ministry; I was very happy and excited about my future. I finally was about to live in a desire I had been praying for and praying about. Life was grand. But then, BAM! All hell broke loose.

*But be ever mindful of the days gone by in which, after you were first spiritually enlightened, you endured a great and painful struggle, Sometimes being yourself a gazingstock, publicly exposed to insults and abuse and distress, and sometimes claiming fellowship and making common cause with others who were so treated.*
*—Hebrews 10:32-33* AMP

Like I said earlier, prior to my test, I was spiritually enlightened, prayers had been answered, and I was standing in a good place, singing with joy in my heart. God was affirming my identity, I was being blessed, and I knew it. But then came a time of testing and trial.

Even Jesus Himself did not escape such testing and trial. In the third chapter of Matthew, Jesus must have seemed at a height, being baptized by John and having his Father call down His affirmations from heaven. Then, in the fourth chapter of Matthew, Jesus is led by the Spirit into the wilderness to be tempted of the devil. (See Matthew 4:1-11,) In a similar way, there I was, being led into a wilderness experience to be tempted to doubt God and His love for me; to be tempted to give up and let fear rule my life.

Before His ministry of healing and teaching took place, and before His preaching took place, and before He opened blind eyes and unstopped deaf ears, before He cast out demons and raised the dead —Jesus had to be tested and tried by temptation.

God was about to use His only begotten Son, so Jesus needed to demonstrate His human capacity, ability and competency to do what He was sent to do.

In a similar way, before we are birthed forth into our best season of ministry, we too must show our capacity, ability and competency to do what God has chose us to do. These are shown in many ways, and one of the most pronounced ways is in how we accept and handle the tests in our lives. Preparation is the key to passing the tests we must take. Jesus prepared Himself by learning and studying as we are told in the book of Luke.

*After three days they found him in the temple, sitting in the midst of the doctors, both hearing them, and asking them questions. And all that heard him were astonished at his understanding and answers. And when they saw him, they were amazed: and his mother said unto him, Son, why hast thou thus dealt with us? behold, thy father and I have sought thee sorrowing. And he said unto them, How is it that ye sought me? wist ye not that I must be about my Father's business?*    *—Luke 2:46-49*

Just as the tree is prepared for winter by dropping its leaves and pulling all of its resources deep into the branches, trunk, and roots for survival, we too must pull all of the Scriptures, songs, prayers, and words deep into our souls for survival during harsh times of testing. This is not a time for growth in your spiritual life; this is a time of standing and maintaining. The roots have to have a sturdy foundation to survive the tests of a winter season. Keep your trust in God no matter what happens.

*Do not, therefore, fling away your fearless confidence, for it carries a
great and glorious compensation of reward.*

—*Hebrews 10:35* AMP

God knows when waiting and standing is needed for a perfect
performance in fulfilling His will. This test in your life and is necessary for excellence. But God is faithful and just to keep His awesome
promises. We must be faithful in standing on His Word, believing
while we wait and stand and endure whatever our wintery season
holds for us.

*For you have need of steadfast patience and endurance, so that you may
perform and fully accomplish the will of God, and thus receive and carry
away [and enjoy to the full] what is promised.*

—*Hebrews 10:36* AMP

When you are being tested, you will feel pressure on every side.
You feel cornered, confused, and hunted down. Just like a boxer in
the arena, we get knocked down, blindsided, and sometimes even
humiliated. The Word says that even though these things occur, resurrection power will show up for the sake of Jesus. Promises have
been made and promises will be kept. Your passing grade is this: tell
yourself and remind yourself of the promises, every hour, every min-
ute, and every second of every day.

*We are hedged in (pressed) on every side [troubled and oppressed in
every way], but not cramped or crushed; we suffer embarrassments and
are perplexed and unable to find a way out, but not driven to despair.
We are pursued (persecuted and hard driven), but not deserted [to stand
alone]; we are struck down to the ground, but never struck out and
destroyed; always carrying about in the body the liability and exposure
to the same putting to death that the Lord Jesus suffered, so that the
[resurrection] life of Jesus also may be shown forth by and in our bodies.*

*For we who live are constantly [experiencing] being handed over to death for Jesus' sake, that the [resurrection] life of Jesus also may be evidenced through our flesh which is liable to death.*
                                     —*2 Corinthians 4:8-11* AMP

For Jesus' sake, we never give up. Our troubles are small compared to what He went through. The hour of our trouble will not last forever; it is going to pass on by. The affliction is testing our commitment and preparing us for greater works. Our inner strength grows stronger every day that we stand and endure.

*Therefore we do not become discouraged (utterly spiritless, exhausted, and wearied out through fear). Though our outer man is [progressively] decaying and wasting away, yet our inner self is being [progressively] renewed day after day. For our light, momentary affliction (this slight distress of the passing hour) is ever more and more abundantly preparing and producing and achieving for us an everlasting weight of glory [beyond all measure, excessively surpassing all comparisons and all calculations, a vast and transcendent glory and blessedness never to cease!].*
                                   —*2 Corinthians 4:16-17* AMP

I like how the *Amplified Bible* describes this weight of glory in those last couple of lines!

Second Corinthians 6:4-10 tells us to "commend ourselves in every way as [true] servants of God." Then it goes on to list many of the attributes of affliction that chosen believers deal with almost every day. Paul adds that we deal with these afflictions through innocence and purity and by speaking the Word of truth in the power of God; "with weapons of righteousness for the right hand [to attack] and for the left hand [to defend]." We do this so that we are approved as blameless ministers of God.

Stand tall in spirit, stand still like a soldier on alert, armed and dangerous. God's Word tells us that this will ensure our resistance to caving in or giving up.

*Therefore put on God's complete armor, that you may be able to resist and stand your ground on the evil day [of danger], and having done all [the crisis demands], to stand [firmly in your place].*
*—Ephesians 6:13* AMP

Test-taking time usually lends itself to the teacher giving instructions beforehand on how to take the test. When a test comes in a believer's life, staying close to God is crucial so that you can hear the instructions He has for you. Sometimes the Lord will tell you to stand quietly and watch as He performs an incredible rescue operation.

*You shall not need to fight in this battle; take your positions, stand still, and see the deliverance of the Lord [Who is] with you, O Judah and Jerusalem. Fear not nor be dismayed. Tomorrow go out against them, for the Lord is with you.*      *—2 Chronicles 20:17* AMP

Obedience to God is crucial. He gives you instructions, strategies, insight, and wisdom. These instructions guide you in every test you must take. God wants to know how far you will go in obeying Him. Think about how a math teacher will give you a formula to solve a problem. They always want you to test the formula out by doing homework. This proves the instructions given. The teacher wants you to hold on to this formula because you will need to have mastered it to pass the upcoming test. First Thessalonians 5:21 tells us to prove all things, to test all things, and to hold fast that which is good. Instructions before a test go a long way, because during the test, the Teacher is always quiet.

*For this was my purpose in writing you, to test your attitude and see
if you would stand the test, whether you are obedient and altogether
agreeable [to following my orders] in everything.*
—*2 Corinthians 2:9* AMP

Even though God affirmed Jesus at His baptism, God still tested
Him. After passing the tests, Jesus returned to Galilee in the power
of the Spirit.

*Jesus returned in the power of the Spirit into Galilee: and there went out
a fame of him through all the region round about.*          —*Luke 4:14*

### Overflow Scripture Meditations

*He said, Hearken, all Judah, you inhabitants of Jerusalem, and you king
Jehoshaphat. The Lord says this to you: be not afraid or dismayed at this
great multitude; for the battle is not yours, but God's.*
—*2 Chronicles 20:15* AMP

*But in all things approving ourselves as the ministers of God, in
much patience, in affliction, in necessities, in distresses, in stripes, in
imprisonments, in tumults, in labors, in watchings, in fastings; by
pureness, by knowledge, by longsuffering, by kindness, by the Holy
Ghost, by love unfeigned, by the word of truth, by the power of God, by
the armor of righteousness on the right hand and on the left, by honor
and dishonor, by evil report and good report: as deceivers, and yet true;
as unknown, and yet well known; as dying, and behold, we live; as
chastened, and not killed; as sorrowful, yet always rejoicing; as poor, yet
making many rich; as having nothing, and yet possessing all things.*
—*2 Corinthians 6:4-10*

# YOU CANNOT HAVE A TESTIMONY WITHOUT A TEST.

*Author Unknown*

# HE CORRECTS THE TEST

*Study to show thyself approved.*                    *—2 Timothy 2:15*

After having taught a particular subject and then administering the test, the teacher then corrects the test. So it is likewise in the spirit. When it is over, God corrects the testing of your spiritual faith Remember, God corrects those that He loves. I remember after taking a test in school, sometimes I couldn't wait to see how well I did, hoping for and expecting an A+. Yet some students did not even want to see their results for fear of receiving an F. Once the teacher began to return the test papers, one by one you would hear the students exclaiming their delight over the grade they received and sharing with one another, "What did you get?" "Oh I got an A, oh wow!" "I got a B+!" "Hey John, what did you get?" "I got a C, and that's great for me! I did better than I did on the last test. Carol how did you do" "Oh, did not study. I got an F."

Who wants to get an F? Prepare yourself for the test, for you know it is coming. Jesus understood preparation. The quality of preparation determines the quality of performance. Jesus never hurried. He did not begin His earthy ministry until He was 30 years old. His ministry was a brief three-and-one half years, but His preparation time was 30 years. He was very sensitive to the seasons of His life. Preparation time is never wasted.

*Jesus increased in wisdom and stature, and in favor with God and man.*
*—Luke 2:52*

Each believer is in a different season of growth in their walk with the Lord. The Parable of the Virgins in Matthew 25:1-13 tells the story of those who were prepared and those who were unprepared to meet the bridegroom. You do not want to be unprepared. Study, meditate, read, and listen. Taking notes in class is always helpful for remembrance, so take notes while attending church, while attending Bible study, while praying, and while studying. Write down promises and verses that speak to you and tape them on a wall in your room or put them on the refrigerator. Make His promises plain and visible.

*I am the True Vine, and My Father is the Vinedresser.*
*—John 15:1* AMP

God will be correcting your test. In school the teacher would always use a red pen to correct the test. There would be a line through the wrong answer, with a note on the side with the correct answer. The red pen would stand out. When you recorded an exceptional answer, you would receive good remarks with a happy face. When you got older, maybe the teacher would put an exclamation point instead. These remarks would cut out the wrong answers or encourage you with praises for good answers.

During correction time, be quiet and listen. God will be doing the talking, He will be speaking to you in order to give you instructions. You may be instructed to take on new subjects like discernment, wisdom, or a class on taming the tongue—whatever He has revealed to you as areas you need more study in.

*Any branch in me that does not bear fruit [that stops bearing] He cuts away (trims off, takes away); and He cleanses and repeatedly prunes every branch that continues to bear fruit, to make it bear more and richer and more excellent fruit.*
*—John 15:2* AMP

The Word also tells us that we are made perfect through suffering. God saw that it was proper and right to allow Jesus to suffer in order to bring vast multitudes into heaven. Jesus is our perfect trailblazer, leading many to salvation. Chosen believers serve God and are His messengers, and therefore must continually receive new strategies for thinking and working. Updates are available on demand. School is never out, and sometimes you may get an easy A. The chosen ones must endure the tough classes as well as the easy ones, though.

*To you it was shown, that you might realize and have personal knowledge that the Lord is God; there is no other besides Him. Out of heaven He made you hear His voice, that He might correct, discipline, and admonish you; and on earth He made you see His great fire, and you heard His words out of the midst of the fire.*
                                          *—Deuteronomy 4:35-36* AMP

When you get to college, you take classes that are required for your advancement in the field you major in. Think of it like that, even when the class is hard, you enroll yourself in it anyway because you know you need it for graduation. If the class is really difficult, you might hire a tutor, or look for a mentor in the class.

*Paul, A bond servant of God and an apostle (a special messenger) of Jesus Christ (the Messiah) to stimulate and promote the faith of God's chosen ones and to lead them on to accurate discernment and recognition of and acquaintance with the Truth which belongs to and harmonizes with and tends to godliness.*          *—Titus 1:1* AMP

When God is correcting you and giving you instructions, humble yourself according to James 4:10, because promotion in life comes from God. Jesus humbled Himself; therefore, God did something according to Philippians 2:9-11. God exalted Jesus to the highest place and gave Him a name above every name. Jesus humbled Himself and God responded. He didn't just exalt Him, but He "exalted Jesus to the highest place." The Scriptures say that promotion in life does not come from men.

*For promotion cometh neither from the east, Nor from the west, nor from the south. But God is the judge: He putteth down one, and setteth up another.*     **—Psalm 75:6-7**

This means that advancement, progress, and development in your life do not come from man's doing, but from God.

## Overflow Scripture Meditations

*O my God, I trust in thee: let me not be ashamed, let not mine enemies triumph over me.*     **—Psalms 25:2**

*For it was an act worthy [of God] and fitting [to the divine nature] that He, for Whose sake and by Whom all things have their existence, in bringing many sons into glory, should make the Pioneer of their salvation perfect [should bring to maturity the human experience necessary to be perfectly equipped for His office as High Priest] through suffering.*     **—Hebrews 2:10** AMP

*There is a way which seems right to a man and appears straight before him, but at the end of it is the way of death.*     **—Proverbs 14:12**

*And it shall be that before they call I will answer; and while they are yet speaking I will hear.*     **—Isaiah 65:24**

*Apply thine heart unto instruction, and thine ears to the words of knowledge.*     **—Proverbs 23:12**

*Poverty and shame shall be to him that refuseth instruction: but he that regardeth reproof shall be honored.*     **—Proverbs 13:18**

WHEN YOU HAVE SUCCESS, IT'S NOT
ABOUT EGO. YOU'RE JUST SAYING,
"THANK YOU GOD, FOR USING ME."

*Indie Arie*

# THE SUN SHINES ON SUNDAY

*For the time being no discipline brings joy, but seems grievous and painful; but afterwards it yields a peaceable fruit of righteousness to those who have been trained by it.* —*Hebrews 12:11* AMP

The exercise of struggle or discipline is difficult and sometimes painful. However God's purpose is to train you and bring you into conformity to His wonderful will in purpose, thought, and action. The result is a chosen and tried believer grown up in favor and character, and perfection. This peaceable fruit of righteousness reminds me of a peaceful day relaxing in a hammock under a shady tree while the sun is shining.

After the hardest part of my struggle, when I actually could see the rising of the sun and had gained some victory, I began to search out the true meaning of all I had endured. The Word tells us to get understanding and I wanted understanding on all levels of what I was coming out of. And like I said before, when you are living to please God, he takes notice and will promote you to a higher place in Him, which means you have gained new access with a shield of favor which allows you to move through your transition of struggle.

*Through Him also we have [our] access (entrance, introduction) by faith into this grace (state of God's favor) in which we [firmly and safely] stand. And let us rejoice and exhult in our hope of experiencing and enjoying the glory of God.* —*Romans 5:2* AMP

Difficult times help to prepare us to minister to the needs of others. The strength we receive when we stand and endure is a salve of healing to those who will hear our testimony. A wise man once said, "Experience is the best teacher." An even wiser woman said, "the best teacher is one who has had the experience and is willing to tell you so you can avoid the pitfalls."

People see Jesus in our lives when we overcome adversity with the power of God. We become parables of Jesus Christ to the people we meet… a greater glimpse of Who God is and the power He gives to stand and endure hardship is shown to others when we successfully weather life's storms. Difficult times build strength in us, strength produces endurance and endurance gives us a better testimony.

*You know we call those blessed (happy) who wee steadfast [who endured]. You have heard of the endurance of Job, and you have seen the Lord's [purpose and how He richly blessed him in the ] end, inasmuch as the Lord is full of pity and compassion and tenderness and mercy.*
*—James 5:11* AMP

At the dawning of a new day, you will receive the crown of life and that is great all by itself. However, there is more: when the sun arises in your situation, it is indeed a new day, a new day that allows you to carry a weight of glory that is everlasting. The promises that God made to you will start showing up. Your compensation of reward will fill you with satisfaction. Being renewed day by day will keep you young and alive. Getting double for your trouble will give you empowerment. When the sun starts to shine for you, it is your time and it is your turn. God sets a certain time for your chosen season.

*You will arise and have mercy and loving-kindness for Zion, for it is time to have pity and compassion for her; yes, the set time has come [the moment designated}.*     *—Psalm 102:13* AMP

After Jesus passed the temptations in the wilderness, He walked on water, changed water to wine, opened blinded eyes, unstopped deaf ears, raised the dead, and casted out demons. After you pass through your wilderness God will anoint you to bring good news to the suffering, the afflicted, and the broken-hearted. You will be able to tell them about beauty for ashes, the joy for mourning and the spirit of praise instead of the spirit of heaviness. You can tell the world how God planted you like a strong and graceful oak tree for His own glory. How God rebuilt you up, when you thought you were destroyed. How future generations have renewed hope. How you have helped to bridge the gap.

*And they shall rebuild the ancient ruins; they shall raise up the former desolations and renew the ruined cities, the devastations of many generations.*                       *—Isaiah 61:4* AMP

When you stand until the end of your salvation, the compensation plan includes benefits for more than just yourself. It includes benefits for many more children of God.

Jesus passed the test and we have reaped the benefits. His glory was greater, His power was stronger, His character was holier, His name was sweeter, His thoughts were higher, His presence was closer, His promises were surer, His foundation was firmer, and His teachings were clearer. Those things happened after Jesus endured a time of testing, trials and tribulation.

When you give thanks to God and offer the sacrifice of praise from the fires of trials and the floods of adversity, the sweetest fragrance is released. God's response to praise ushers you into worship. Your worship experience may cause tears to stream down your face, to dance all over the floor and take off running. So by all means give God the glory.

Influence flows from intimacy, so as you develop intimacy with your Father which art in heaven, you will have a measure of influence over the lives of people who hear your testimony. Access comes from relationship, and as you develop your relationship with God the Father, you will gain more and more access into new territory.

Now I am laughing; now I am singing; now I am dreaming. God will do amazing things in your life. He will give you wonderful surprises and unexpected gifts. You will begin to experience the serendipities of life. Yes! Glorious things to refresh you with. When you have sown your seeds of faith in standing, you shall reap a harvest of joy.

*When the Lord brought back the captives to Zion we were like them that dream [it seems so unreal]. Then were our mouths filled with laughter, and our tongues with singing. Then they said among the nations, the Lord has done great things for them. The Lord has done great things for us! We are glad! Turn the freedom of our captivity and restore our fortunes, O Lord.*                   —*Psalm 126:1-4a* AMP

One of the prerequisites for seeing the sun is praying for your friends even though they may have doubted you all along your tribulation and offered you bad advice. Another prerequisite for seeing the sun shine is forgiving one another for trespasses. When you engage in this behavior, God will restore you and give you double for your trouble.

*When Job prayed for his friends, the Lord restored his fortunes. In fact, the Lord gave him twice as much as before!*            —*Job 42:10* NLT

Now that the sun has begun to arise in your life, celebrate! A celebration comes with victory. With a celebration come gifts from family and friends. Also with this celebration comes a feast. Eat drink and be merry.

*Then there came to him all his brothers and sisters and all who had known him before, and they ate bread with him in his house; and they sympathized with him and comforted him over all the distressing calamities that the Lord had brought upon him. Every man also gave him a piece of money, and every man an earring of gold.* —*Job 42:11*

A sun-day brings you into abundance and overflow. Simply put, you get more. More of everything becomes available at the dawning of a new day. When the sun arises, you will be inspired to righteousness.

*And the Lord blessed the latter days of Job more than his beginning*
*—Job 42:12a*

Take a look back to where you came from and consider the deliverance you received from God. Take a look at how you thought you were not going to make it and remember the blessing.

Once you have received victory after a struggle, comfort and restoration are next. You have made it through and the sun is shinning for you.

*For the Lord will comfort Zion; He will comfort her waste places. And He will make her wilderness like Eden, and her desert like the garden of the Lord. Joy and gladness will be found in her, thanksgiving and the voice of song or instrument of praise.*          *—Isaiah 51:3* AMP

Let's look at the book of Esther and see another recorded celebration of victory. Esther was chosen to work with God in achieving victory over Haman and his evil plot against His people. I will show you how even on sun-day, when the sun is shinning, God will ask you if you want more of His deliverance.

Esther displayed a killer instinct when it came to victory. While enjoying her sun-day, the king asked her "what more do you want." She indeed wanted more. When God asks you "what more do you want?' Always reply "complete victory."

Learning from the book of Esther – God will give you an extra day to make sure your victory is complete! God will give you an extra day to annihilate the enemy.

The wisdom of the King will use the same process that elevates you, to humiliate and annihilate the enemy i.e. The Red Sea. (Exodus)

**Complete** = what you do not eradicate when you are strong will come back to attack you later. "Do not let the sun go down on your wrath" finish the fight! It is up to us in our day to bring closure and to destroy the lingering works of the enemy. David slew Goliath and then he took Goliath's sword and cut his head off. That is complete victory! You can find that story in 1Samuel 17:1-51. The Red sea was forced back by a strong east wind to allow the Jews to cross on dry ground (sun-day). When Moses stretched forth his hand a second time over the Sea the waters returned and drowned the Egyptians. Complete Victory! In another case we see that God wanted Saul to eradicate the Amalekites, God wanted complete victory over these people. Saul left king Agag alive and the best sheep and oxen, in other words he disobeyed God. This caused him to loose his kingship. 500 years later Esther is dealing with Haman- an Agagite. See 1Samuel 15:3 and verses 9-11. Adopt Esther's tactics. When the king asked Esther what more did she request, she responded by asking for Haman's ten sons to be hanged. Complete Victory! We must use the 'Signet ring' of the King's name (Jesus) while wearing the garment of praise, worship and righteousness.

*For the weapons of our warfare are not physical, but they are mighty before God for the overthrow and destruction of strongholds, [in as much as we] refuse arguments and theories and reasoning's and every proud and lofty thing that sets itself up against the [true] knowledge of God; and we lead every thought and purpose away captive into the obedience of Christ. Being in readiness to punish every disobedience, when your own submission and obedience are fully secured and complete.*

—*2 Corinthians 10:4-6* AMP

Notice how this scripture tells you the prerequisite for complete victory is in your obedience as a believer. Completion comes after (obedience during a struggle). As long as you tolerate sin within the palace, it multiplies. You must eradicate the enemy in your day of strength. Esther's story is the ultimate journal of divine reversal (see Esther 8:5).

**Victory** = celebrate these days with feasting and gladness and by giving gifts to each other and to the poor.

*As the day on which the Jews got rest from their enemies. And as the month which was turned for them from sorrow to gladness and from mourning into a holiday-that they should make them days of feasting and gladness, days of sending choice portions to one another and gifts to the poor.*                          —*Esther 9:22* AMP

They had a two day celebration.

*You prepare a feast for me in the presence of my enemies. You welcome me as a guest, anointing my head with oil. My cup overflows with blessings.*                          —*Psalm 23:5* NLT

### Overflow Scripture Meditations

*Therefore they shall come and sing in the height of Zion, and shall flow together to the goodness of the Lord, for wheat, and for wine, and for oil, and for the young of the flock and of the herd: and their soul shall be as a watered garden; and they shall not sorrow any more at all.*
                          —*Jeremiah 31:12*

*Hearken to me, you who follow after rightness and justice, you who seek and inquire of [and require] the Lord [claiming Him by necessity and by right]: look to the rock from which you were hewn and to the hole in*

*he quarry from which you were dug; look to Abraham your father and to Sarah who bore you; for I called him when he was yet but one, and I blessed him and made him many.*     **—Isaiah 51:1-2** AMP

*Arise, Shine; for thy light is come, and the glory of the Lord is risen upon thee.*     **—Isaiah 60:1-22**

A WISE MAN ONCE SAID, "EXPERIENCE IS THE BEST TEACHER." AN EVEN WISER WOMAN SAID, "THE BEST TEACHER IS ONE WHO HAS HAD THE EXPERIENCE AND IS WILLING TO TELL YOU SO YOU CAN AVOID THE PITFALLS."

*Millicent Hunter*

# NEW AND SHARP INSTRUMENT

*Behold, I will make you to be a new, sharp, threshing instrument which
has teeth; you shall thresh the mountains and beat them small, and shall
make the hills like chaff. You shall winnow them, and the wind shall
carry them away, and the tempest or whirlwind shall scatter them. And
you shall rejoice in the Lord, you shall glory in the Holy One of Israel.*
*—Isaiah 41:15-16* AMP

When God makes you a new, sharp, threshing instrument with
teeth, nothing shall be impenetrable to you. Things will have to move
out of your way. Mountains of problems and hills of hindrance will
no longer be a threat. "New and sharp" means you have been rede-
fined and fine-tuned. Your spirit will remain winsome even through
heartache, tears, and standing at death's door. This new you will produce a change in your walk and a change in your talk. A brand new
you shall now have access to new territory and new dimensions. Now
you have a new song to sing. After you have been through the fire
and through the flood, signs and wonders will start following you. As
Deuteronomy 28:7 tells us, the enemy will flee from you seven ways.

You shall be a cut above, ten times better than the rest, just as
Daniel was. (See Daniel 1:20.) Greater is He that is in you than he
that is in the world.

You are called into this grace in which you stand; other people
couldn't stand in the same place. You were chosen to go first because
you were strong enough. Remember, He does not put more on you
than you can stand or bare.

As you stand firmly in your place, having tightened the belt of
truth around your loins; having put on the breastplate of integrity,
moral rectitude, and right standing with God; having shod your feet
in preparation, ready to face the enemy with firm-footed stability

because of the good news; you will have influence! You can affect change in the lives of those who are bound and held hostage. Amen!

God will give you previews of coming attractions, allowing you to taste and see His goodness and His plans to prosper you. You will walk in unexplained favor. Grace, truth, goodness, and mercy will be your bodyguards. People will be mesmerized by the signs and wonders following you, because we serve an awesome God.

Your future comes one day at a time. It is God's present to you. Every moment of every day, with every thought you think and every word you speak, makes a decision to move you toward greatness. Prepare yourself for every good work; build on your experiences, adding to your faith as you develop godly ability and character. You are new wine now, and you have been given a new wineskin. God is forming new roads for you to travel. Your soul is now more resilient and hardened to difficulties.

When we get to the point where we can thrive in the midst of adversity, we are like the evergreens that have learned to be majestic in every season. The seasons pass, but our branches are always green. The pruning comes, but our sap is thick, sticky, and sweet—we heal fast. Spring, summer, fall, or winter, our branches spread to glorify the King of Kings while we shelter others from the harsh winds of winter and offer shade from the summer heat. The fruit we bear is full of seeds, falling to the ground, and giving birth to new seedlings.

*Blessed is the man. . . His leaf also shall not wither; And whatsoever he doeth shall prosper.*     **—Psalm 1:1,3**

The Bible says that we are the salt of the earth and we have the light of life living within us. The earth has flavor because we are in it. We shed light in dark places.

We are to be salted by the fire of the trials we go through so that we may be able to handle the weight of glory. (See Mark 9:49.) The weight is heavy, and we build spiritual muscles by our standing endurance and obedience. Shake your salt and shine your light every chance you get. The Scriptures tell us to always let our speech be gracious, seasoned with salt that we may know how we should answer ever man. (See Colossians 4:6.) When you know the promise, the price is easy.

*And Jesus returned in the power of the Spirit into Galilee: and there went out a fame of him through the entire region round about. . . . And the eyes of all them that were in the synagogue were fastened on him. And he began to say unto them, This day is this scripture fulfilled in your ears.*
—*Luke 4:14; 20-21*

Doors that need to be opened will be opened and things that need to happen will happen without your having to push, pull, or tug. You will simply stand back and watch God perform. God will bring everything and everybody that you need into your life. You will attract people with divinely ordained assignments, which will have just the talents you need to carry out the work He has assigned to you. Hallelujah!

*I will give thee thanks in the great congregation: I will praise thee among much people.*     —*Psalm 35:18*

You will see that prayers you prayed long ago are answered. You will see that intercessions you offered for others are happening. You will see that all things work together for good because you love the Lord.

I encourage you to write your prayer seeds down so that you have a reference point from which to count your blessings and to give God glory and honor. When you see the seeds you have planted come to fruition, you know its your time to shine.

You will be laughing at the devil. Laughter will fill your life because you will be able to look back and see God's purpose. There will be a smile on your face and you will certainly know that the victory is yours for the taking. The joy of the Lord will be your strength. (See Nehemiah 8:10.) You will rejoice with joy unspeakable. (See Peter 1:8b.) You will experience His joy, and your joy will be full. (See John 15:11.) You will have tremendous respect and love for God's Word.

In this new season, stay watchful, because as you release and nurture joy, spiritual warfare will become very subtle. In the midst of the blessing, the enemy likes to tell us, "Look at what you have accomplished. See how much you are doing for the kingdom of God? My, what a wonderful Christian you have become. Forget the past, forget the pain—sit back and enjoy the good life you have now." But you want to be able to call up the memories of the past. You don't want to forget what you have come through. This is yet another tactic of the enemy. New levels bring new devils. You want to remember where you have come from and that God has brought you to this point.

Spiritually, I think it is important for us to keep the memories of our adversities fresh. If we get to the point that we forget, we desensitize ourselves. Then we cannot identify with what other people in pain are feeling. We need to be able to minister to them on a deep level, to look them in the eyes, connect with their pain, and tell them, "Oh yes, you can make it. I know, because I was once right where you are right now."

We must stay aware that the enemy will come in with this subtle deception. He wants us to forget where we came from. We must not. We must give our testimony of overcoming with praise, thanksgiving, and glory to God for all that He brought us through. Israel recounted the sufferings of the people and the deliverance of God from generation to generation; we should do the same.

God will always have people who stand strong for Him, a remnant who love Him. I believe He is using the purging of the seasons to sift out this remnant. You have been chosen to prevail.

*And I will bring the third part through fire, And will refine them as silver is refined, And will try them as gold is tried: They shall call on my name, and I will hear them: I will say, It is my people: And they shall say, The LORD is my God.*     —*Zechariah 13:9*

Now you can minister hope to those that are in the midst of adversity. The words of your testimony will have life and power. The blood of Christ gives every word life, and so the message lives. I have entered a season of continuous praise for what God has done in my life. I stood tall and survived. I came out of the valley. I weathered the storm. The smile on my face is genuine. The love in my heart is sincere. The excitement with which I serve God is real. I have no doubt that your reading of this book is no accident. I believe it is to encourage you during your affliction.

Suffering in and of itself is not a privilege. However, when we suffer as a result of faithfully representing Christ, we know that our message and example have an effect. We know that God considers us worthy to represent Him. Suffering for our faith does not mean we have done something wrong. In fact, the opposite is often true—it verifies that we have been faithful.

*But none of these things move me, neither count I my life dear unto myself, so that I might finish my course with joy, and the ministry, which I have received of the Lord Jesus, to testify the gospel of the grace of God*     —*Acts 20:24*

When everything about you has changed for the better and your name is associated with nobility, there will be this one thing to remind you to remain humble.

*Even though I have received such wonderful revelations from God. So to keep me from becoming proud, I was given a thorn in my flesh, a messenger from Satan to torment me and keep me from becoming proud.*
　　　　　　　　　　　　　　　　　　　—*2 Corinthians 12:7* NLT

He goes on to explain how he wanted to be free from this humbling thing.

*Three times I pleaded with the Lord to take it away from me.*
　　　　　　　　　　　　　　　　　　　—*2 Corinthians 12:8* NIV

And God did send him an answer: GRACE!

*But He said to me, My grace (My favor and loving-kindness and mercy) is enough for you [sufficient against any danger and enables you to bear the trouble manfully]; for My strength and power are made perfect (fulfilled and completed) and show themselves most effective in [your] weakness.*　　　　　　　　　　　　—*2 Corinthians 12:9* AMP

After having heard and understood this response, Paul decided to submit to God on this matter. He came to understand that grace is divine power and that this power meant favor, love, and forgiveness against the thorn in his flesh. Ephesians 2:7 tells us that this grace is a free gift from God and that it is full of riches. One rich aspect of grace is that it saved us through our faith in Jesus Christ. The Holy Spirit ministers grace to us from God to save us and enable us to live holy lives and to accomplish the will of God. According to Hebrews 12:28, we need grace in order to serve God. Now you should feel tremendously powerful, because you have reached a point in life where your personality is aligned with what your soul came to do.

*Therefore, I will all the more gladly glory in my weaknesses and infirmities, that the strength and power of Christ (the Messiah) may rest (yes, may pitch a tent over and dwell) upon me!*
*—2 Corinthians 12:9b* AMP

Titus 2:11-12 tells us that grace trains us in how to serve and live holy. Grace has appeared for the deliverance of sin and for eternal salvation, isn't that awesome?

*For the eyes of the* Lord *run to and fro throughout the whole earth, to show Himself strong in the behalf of them whose heart is perfect toward him.*     *—2 Chronicles 16:9*

Pearls are beautiful and lovely to look at, but did you know that pearls are the product of irritation? This irritation occurs when the shell of the oyster is invaded by an alien substance like a grain of sand. When that happens, all the resources within the tiny, sensitive oyster rush to the irritant spot and begin to release healing fluids. By and by the irritation is covered with this substance until it becomes a pearl. Had there been no irritation, there would be no pearl. No wonder our heavenly home has pearly gates to welcome the wounded and bruised!

*When the enemy shall come in like a flood, the Spirit of the* Lord *shall lift up a standard against him.*     *—Isaiah 59:19b*

You have become an empowerment leader. Old things have passed away, all things have become new. You will have a fresh excitement, a fresh mind, and a fresh zeal for the Lord. The new you will be uncontaminated and uncompromised. You now have better discernment and you conduct your affairs expeditiously. Your feet will be as hind's feet over all your troubles. In Genesis 45:8, Joseph says "You did not put me here, God did." Verse 7 says, "I had to go before you I so could save you a posterity in the earth."

*But ye shall be named the Priests of the LORD: Men shall call you the Ministers of our God: Ye shall eat the riches of the Gentiles, And in their glory shall ye boast yourselves.*    —*Isaiah 61:6*

Great grace is great power. According to Acts 4:33, this great grace gave the apostles the ability to deliver their testimonies to the resurrection of Jesus Christ. The Scripture tells us that this great grace rested richly upon them.

*And I will give you pastors according to mine heart, which shall feed you with knowledge and understanding.*    —*Jeremiah 3:15*

To gain understanding is powerful. Understanding at its core, gives you revelation. The divine power of revelation is equal to truly seeing "the light" or grasping spiritual truth. When you can truly see spiritual truth, then you really have the knowledge of the truth. Jesus, in all His teaching, gives us the ability to see the true light through chosen leaders. Jesus is the True Light that gives light to every human being.

This light causes you to do damage in darkness. The hedge of protection around you and all that is assigned to you shall be strengthened by God. God assigned angels as your divine escorts and supernatural security guards. Evil will be dismantled and scattered. You have been given a massive invisible army of angels to serve and to minister. Once God opens heaven for you, you will see the activity of the angels ascending and descending. (See John 1:51 and Genesis 28:12.)

Being free, fearless, and bold in the Lord continues to bear witness to the word of grace, which is the word of divine power. It is this power that allows you to perform signs and wonders. (See Acts 14:3.)

*And he said, Behold, I make a covenant: before all thy people I will do marvels, such as have not been done in all the earth, nor in any nation: and all the people among which thou art shall see the work of the LORD: for it is a terrible thing that I will do with thee.*     **—Exodus 34:10**

The macadamia tree takes 20 years to grow and it produces fruit—nuts—for over 100 years. The blessing will continue for many generations—think about the marvel of that!

*Verily, verily, I say unto you, He that believeth on me, the works I do shall he do also; and greater works than these shall he do; because I go to my Father.*     **—John 14:12**

Because Jesus had to go to the Father and sit down at His right hand, we are left to do greater works under the protection and care of God who also gives us the Word of His grace, which is divine favor from divine power. (See Acts 20:32.)

*It is the glory of God to conceal a thing: But the honor of kings is to search out a matter.*     **—Proverbs 25:2**

Unlocking the mystery is an honor. We are supposed to search for the secret things God has concealed for His glory. Jesus came to help us solve the mysteries in our lives by giving us knowledge. He came to let us know what's really going on. That is why God wants us to pursue, chase, go after, and hunt for wisdom and understanding above all else. (See Proverbs 4:5-7.)

*Through wisdom is an house builded; And by understanding it is established: And by knowledge shall the chambers be filled With all precious and pleasant riches.*     **—Proverbs 24:3-4**

*Make every effort to keep the unity of the Spirit through the bond of peace. There is one body and one Spirit, just as you were called to one hope when you were called; one Lord, one faith, one baptism; one God and Father of all, who is over all and through all and in all.*

    **—Ephesians 4:3-6** NIV

Verse 7 of this passage tells us that there will be grace according to the measure of the gift of Christ. First Peter 4:10 says each one should use whatever gift he has received to serve others, faithfully administering God's grace in its various forms.

*Remember now thy Creator in the days of thy youth, while the evil days come not, nor the years draw nigh, when thou shalt say, I have no pleasure in them.*     **—Ecclesiastes 12:1**

*And moreover, because the preacher was wise, he still taught the people knowledge; yea, he gave good heed, and sought out, and set in order many proverbs. The preacher sought to find out acceptable words: and that which was written was upright, even words of truth.*

    **—Ecclesiastes 12:9-10**

You are to be busy promoting and populating the kingdom of God. Clothe yourself as God's own chosen ones—put on love, which is the bond of perfectness.

*I am watching to see that my word is fulfilled.*  **—Jeremiah 1:12** NIV

*And the child grew, and waxed strong in spirit, filled with wisdom: and the grace of God was upon him.*     **—Luke 2:40**

## Overflow Scripture Meditations

*Therefore, my beloved brethren, be ye steadfast, unmovable, always abounding in the work of the Lord, forasmuch as ye know that your labor is not in vain in the Lord*        **—1 Corinthians 15:58**

*The steps of a good man are ordered by the LORD: And He delighted in his way. Though he fall, he shall not be utterly be cast down: For the LORD upholdeth him with his hand.*        **—Psalm 37:23-24**

*And all these blessings shall come upon thee, and overtake thee, if thou shalt hearken unto the voice of the LORD thy God. . . . And the LORD shall make thee the head, and not the tail; and thou shalt be above only, and thou shalt not be beneath; if that thou hearken unto the commandments of the LORD thy God, which I command thee this day, to observe and to do them.*        **—Deuteronomy 28:2, 13**

*The Spirit of the Lord God is upon me, because the Lord has anointed me to bring good news to the suffering and afflicted. He has sent me to comfort the broken-hearted, to announce liberty to the captives and to open the eyes of the blind. He has sent me to tell those who mourn that the time of God's favor to them has come, and the day of his wrath to their enemies. To all who mourn in Israel He will give: Beauty for ashes; Joy instead of mourning; Praise instead of heaviness. For God has planted them like strong and graceful oaks for his own glory.*        **—Isaiah 61:1-3 TLB**

*I know thy works: behold, I have set before thee an open door, and no man can shut it: for thou hast a little strength, and hast kept my word, and hast not denied my name. Behold, I will make them of the synagogue of Satan, which say they are Jews, and are not, but do lie; behold, I will make them to come and worship before thy feet, and to know that I have loved thee.*     **—Revelation 3:8-9**

*But ye are a chosen generation, a royal priesthood, an holy nation, a peculiar people; that ye should show forth the praises of him who hath called you out of darkness into his marvellous light.*     **—1 Peter 2:9**

*I press on to take hold of that for which Christ Jesus took hold of me. Brothers and sisters, I do not consider myself yet to have taken hold of it. But one thing I do: Forgetting what is behind and straining toward what is ahead, I press on toward the goal to win the prize for which God has called me heavenward in Christ Jesus.*     **—Philippians 3:12-14** NIV

*Though he were a Son, yet learned he obedience by the things which he suffered; And being made perfect, he became the author of eternal salvation unto all them that obey him.*     **—Hebrews 5:8-9**

*Humble yourselves in the sight of the Lord, and he shall lift you up.*     **—James 4:10**

*For promotion cometh neither from the east, Nor from the west, nor from the south. But God is the judge: He putteth down one, and setteth up another.*     **—Psalm 75:6-7**

*But Saul increased the more in strength, and confounded the Jews which dwelt at Damascus, proving that this is very Christ.*     **—Acts 9:22**

*Praise ye the* LORD. *I will praise the* LORD *with my whole heart, in the assembly of the upright, and in the congregation.* —**Psalm 111:1**

*And the seventh angel sounded; and there were great voices in heaven, saying, The kingdoms of this world are become the kingdoms of our Lord, and of His Christ; and he shall reign for ever and ever.*

—**Revelation 11:15**

# Recommended Investments

Chosen in the Furnace of Affliction
*by Dr. Juanita Bynum*

Your Promise of Protection
*by Gloria Copeland*

Don't Die in the Winter
*by Millicent Hunter*

Hope for Today (mini book)
*by Joel Osteen*

The Rules of Engagement
*by Cindy Trimm*

Hadassah: One Night with the King
*by Tommy Tenney*

Tried & Chosen

Terri Michelle Hutchinson

**For more Empowerment visit:**

light-of-lifeministries.org

Subscribe to my channel
Terri Michelle Hutchinson

Like my fan page@ lolministries1

www.ingramcontent.com/pod-product-compliance
Lightning Source LLC
LaVergne TN
LVHW051101080426
835508LV00019B/1995